'SSS, is a triumph, a great read, [...] laughing at myself and learning [...] be a better man—generous, courageous and intelligent!'

—**Matt Church**, Founder of Thought Leaders Global and author of *Amplifiers*

'How refreshing to have a book that cuts through the myths and hype and gets to the heart of human behaviour and the realities of why we do what we do. Dan and Kieran share a rare quality of not only being brilliant researchers and strategists, but also being able to translate what they do into what we need to know. And they do it with such a fabulous sense of wit and humour that you can't help but turn the page. This book will change how you view behaviour, business, leadership and even society, forever.'

—**Megan Dalla-Camina**, Strategist and author of *Getting Real About Having It All*

'Clever, rigorous and refreshingly real—this fad-free book shows modern-day realists how to unlock real results.'

—**Dr Jason Fox**, Motivational Scientist and author of *The Game Changer*

'Finally someone has the guts to tell the truth! This book will blow your mind and not allow you to look at the world the same. By removing your blinders it will save you time and help you get what you want.'

—**Dr Adam Fraser**, Human Performance Researcher and author of *The Third Space*

'As business leaders we think we know but Dan and Kieran really know what makes buyers do what they do. Buy this book to find out how to get them to buy more.'

—**Jeffrey Hayzlett**, Primetime TV Show Host, best-selling author and sometime cowboy

'Clever, funny, thoughtful and passionate about success ... the book is too.'

—**Russel Howcroft**, Executive General Manager, Network Ten

'I deeply resent Dan and Kieran's hilariously blunt insights into my human failings—or at least I would—if the opportunity to profit from them wasn't so genuine and compelling. Steel-toed honesty coupled with brilliant original perspectives: Whether your focus is business or philanthropy, this is a book for people who have the courage to understand themselves in order to change the world.'

—**Bradley Trevor Greive AM**, *New York Times* best-selling author

'Dan and Kieran's latest book combines the art of engaging readability with the science of killing sacred cows. This book cuts through the clutter and the rah rah and creates a new paradigm of understanding of human nature, which is essential to create organisations and brands well positioned for a future that isn't just about hype, but about depth and meaning. Hoover it now!'

—**Anders Sörman-Nilsson**, Futurist and Founder of the think tank—Thinque

SELFISH, SCARED & STUPID

SELFISH, SCARED & STUPID

STOP FIGHTING HUMAN NATURE AND INCREASE
YOUR PERFORMANCE, ENGAGEMENT AND INFLUENCE

DAN GREGORY & KIERAN FLANAGAN

WILEY

First published in 2015 by John Wiley & Sons Australia, Ltd
42 McDougall St, Milton Qld 4064

Office also in Melbourne

Typeset in 11/13.5 pt Goudy Oldstyle Std

© The Impossible Institute Pty Ltd 2014

The moral rights of the authors have been asserted

National Library of Australia Cataloguing-in-Publication data:

Author:	Gregory, Dan, author.
Title:	Selfish, scared & stupid: stop fighting human nature and increase your performance, engagement and influence / Dan Gregory, Kieran Flanagan.
ISBN:	9780730312789 (pbk.)
	9780730312796 (ebook)
Notes:	Includes index.
Subjects:	Human behavior.
	Philosophical anthropology.
	Success.
	Conduct of life.
	Social interaction.
Other Authors/ Contributors:	Flanagan, Kieran, author.
Dewey Number:	128

Cover design by Steve York, Cream Studios

Title block and heads graphic © The Impossible Institute

Back cover image by Ian Butterworth

Printed in Singapore by C.O.S. Printers Pte Ltd

10 9 8 7 6 5 4 3 2 1

Disclaimer
The material in this publication is of the nature of general comment only, and does not represent professional advice. It is not intended to provide specific guidance for particular circumstances and it should not be relied on as the basis for any decision to take action or not take action on any matter which it covers. Readers should obtain professional advice where appropriate, before making any such decision. To the maximum extent permitted by law, the authors and publisher disclaim all responsibility and liability to any person, arising directly or indirectly from any person taking or not taking action based on the information in this publication.

*To Kerryanne, Gary and Darcy, the least selfish,
scared and stupid people we know.*

CONTENTS

ABOUT THE AUTHORS

Dan Gregory and Kieran Flanagan are behavioural researchers and strategists and the founders of The Impossible Institute™, an innovation and engagement think-tank founded 'to make what's not ... possible!'

Their specialisation is human behaviour and belief systems — our motives, our drives, the things that make us buy and the things that make us buy in.

Over the past 25 years they have helped develop new product lines for Coca-Cola and Unilever, invented new media formats for Murdoch Magazines, created interaction systems for categories as diverse as fast-food chains and government departments, and launched internal and external engagement campaigns for companies as varied as News Ltd, Vodafone and MTV.

They have also worked as directors and lecturers at Australia's premier creative school, AWARD, lectured at the Miami Ad School, taught postgraduate students at Macquarie University, Sydney and the University of Sydney as well as privately coaching and mentoring CEOs and non-executive board members.

Dan and Kieran are also captivating speakers whose business acumen is matched by a rapier wit and rare human insight — skills that Dan puts to great use in front of 1.4 million viewers as a regular on ABC TV's *Gruen Planet*.

Their mission is to turn Impossible Thinking™ into an epidemic.

ACKNOWLEDGEMENTS

An enormous thank you to our amazingly supportive families, who not only allow us to be selfish, scared and stupid with our time but have also been the collaborators who helped us navigate the world of human behaviour successfully. Special thanks to Kerryanne Gregory, Gary Fishburn, Darcy Fishburn, Lillah and Brian Gregory, Toni and Mike Flanagan, Bruce Gregory, Jodie Coates, Simone Carton, Bronwyn Flanagan, George Betsis and Mary Coustas, and Andy and Trish Healy. We love you all and you make the journey more interesting and a lot more fun.

We also want to thank the amazing colleagues and mentors who have shared the ups and downs of our business lives over the years and contributed in their own way to the writing of this book — Matt Church, Adam Fraser, Julie Winterbottom, Leanne Christie, Heidi Gregory, Tanja Markovic, Rebecca Tapp, Lauren Kelly, Siimon Reynolds, Bradley Trevor Greive and Marty Wilson.

Last, but not least, thank you to the extraordinary team around us who helped to bring this book to fruition: Mathew Alderson, Kristen Hammond, Chris Shorten, Sandra Balonyi, Peter Reardon, Ian Butterworth, Steve York, Felipe Neves, Phaedra Fuller and Sharon Zeev Poole.

INTRODUCTION

Why did you pick up this book or even decide you wanted to read something? Why did you choose your career, your employees, your belief systems, your partner? Seriously, what were you thinking, given most of the people you dated over the years? If ever you needed proof that we don't truly understand what drives us or the people around us, you need only reach for the nearest photo album or trawl through a Facebook archive for a montage of poorly thought-through relationship decisions, ridiculous fashion choices and some cringe-worthy opinions: 'unlike'!

Given all of us are merely the sum total of our decisions, perhaps a better understanding of what drives these decisions, what makes us buy and buy in, is called for. This is particularly pertinent as many of the theories about human behaviour that are doing the rounds are rather flawed and tend to be based more on wishful thinking than experience.

If we're completely honest, for the past 100 years—perhaps throughout most of our history—the focus of understanding what drives human behaviour (or behavioural research, as it is currently known) has been searching for levers, both psychological and physical, with which to influence, change and attempt to control people's behaviour. The aim is to make us more obedient followers, better behaved children, and more productive workers and members of society; and, as our society has industrialised and advanced, more willing consumers and more highly performing teams and individuals. These levers have included some pretty grotesque options over the years, such as coercion, torture, kidnap, stand-over tactics and even slavery. Occupational health and safety is not something the Egyptians, Mesopotamians, Romans or even Dickensians were particularly famous for.

The bulk of this effort has met with mixed success as models of persuasion have come and gone, and human beings have proved to be rather more stuck in our ways and less controllable than we had previously assumed. We are not machines, and trying to alter our behaviour is no easy undertaking.

However, this tendency, rather than signifying failure, has actually armed those of us who work in behavioural research and strategy with a better understanding of what makes the human animal tick, and in fact, it has become quite an asset in this regard.

Having observed all this, it is still true even today, that we do rather romanticise human behaviour, preferring to see the world of motivation, if not through rose-coloured glasses, through glasses tinted with positivism. We like to think that we are motivated by noble thoughts, selfless generosity, a courageous sense of adventure and a capacity to embrace complexity and work tirelessly to achieve success. (How's that working for you?) But of course *we* are; it's just everyone else who needs to lift their game!

This line of thinking is not only largely untrue, highly unrealistic and completely unsustainable, we'll argue that it is in fact counter-productive. It ignores the power within our natural inclinations and ultimately sets us up for failure. What this 'happy delusion' robs us of is a fuller appreciation of who we really are (against the sage advice of Socrates in the quote at the beginning of this chapter); it denies us a broad absolution from what many of us may describe as failings as well as access to strategies based in realities, not academic theory or even the ever-popular pop psychology.

Those of us who lead, who seek to influence, to create change, to sell, to educate or simply to push ourselves and our performance may benefit greatly from a more objective appraisal of the forces that drive our behaviour and some real-world strategies to make us more attractive, motivating, influential, persuasive and successful.

In this book, we'd like to suggest that a strategy based on swimming with the current of human nature, fitting processes to people and enabling individuals and teams to bring the best of who they are (not just who we want them to be) to the table is far more productive and successful than the strategies we currently employ. In an effort to maintain absolute control, our current strategies reduce our efficiency and enthusiasm, and limit our capacity to fully harness our skillsets and talents.

WHO WE ARE AND HOW WE CAME TO WRITE THIS BOOK

For much of our professional lives, we have worked as strategic and creative leaders in what may be described as the world's largest psychological experiment—the advertising industry. Certainly advertising has access to research, sample sizes and cross-cultural results that the academic and clinical worlds cannot come close to. Nor have we been limited, occasionally to our shame, by issues such as ethics, conscience or a moral compass (whatever that is).

However, this has, for the most part, allowed us a great impartiality in our work, an almost sociopathic detachment from values and judgements that may distort the interpretation of results. Quite ironically, it has also provided us with the ability to focus more on the 'truth'.

In our current business—The Impossible Institute, an innovation, engagement and leadership think tank—we now work in the worlds of training, speaking, and cultural engagement and development. Here, too, we have focused more on achieving results than trying to restrict how these results are achieved to fit with our values, prejudices or personal views of the world. It is not our goal to recreate the world in our own image (at least we don't like to admit to that in public).

However, it would be wrong to assume that this 'results focus' is synonymous within the commercial world—it is quite the contrary, in fact. We had assumed that moving from the cloistered worlds of school and university education into the commercial world would enable us to focus more on results and the accumulation of hard data from which we could extrapolate meaning and process. We expected a greater 'bottom-line' emphasis versus the more methodological tendencies of the academic world we all grew up in. It surprised us that this was not the case at all.

The commercial world does, of course, want to lead, influence and persuade both its staff and its customers. It also clearly wants bottom-line results. However, it is also oddly obsessed with the need to control and dictate how these results are achieved. In other words, it wants to be both rich and right, a conflict that not only limits success but also prejudices people's capacity and willingness to contribute to society as a whole.

While we don't wish to appear too Machiavellian in our description of ourselves, neither do we want to suggest that the existing system is quite as noble as it may like to portray itself. What we have found is that our current systems of leadership and process for building cultures and performance are far more judgemental and limiting, and in fact, more values biased than they may first appear.

This tendency to want to control 'how' a result is achieved, and hence people's behaviour and process, as opposed to aligning the result with the values and the pre-existing motivations of the people involved, turns out to be immensely frustrating, not simply for the people involved in the process, but also for the people leading them, their co-workers, customers, students and other people working around them.

What's perhaps more disturbing is that this practice of forcing people to conform to unnatural processes at odds with human nature is virtually universal. We have witnessed it in clients on almost every continent; in every business, educational and government sector; and in innovation projects, cultural audits, personal development and the coaching and mentoring we conduct with leaders of various genders, cultures, ages and persuasions.

In fact, this pattern of trying to create change in line with an imagined 'noble intent' has actually led to some pretty awful, large-scale and ignoble results.

This leads us to the central question of this book.

WHAT REALLY DRIVES HUMAN BEHAVIOUR?

In answering this question, our approach has tended more towards quantitative research than qualitative, though both have informed our conclusions. We have relied less on what human beings *say* and focused more on what they *do* so as not to be biased by our own values or expectations — or theirs. This being said, we have as much as possible tried to include research and case studies from our own experience and what we have gained first hand rather than relying exclusively on the work of others. We have also resisted the temptation to frame our results in the classic 'Top 10 tips to be totally terrific and thoroughly influential' format, preferring instead to outline three core principles that work more like a series of combination locks that are interconnected with each other. These locks can be tweaked, adjusted and personalised as required.

In doing so, our aim is that this book supports a perceptual and behavioural change that offers you, our readers, points of view that you have not previously had access to. Along with these perspectives we wish to arm you with a more holistic and integrated understand of human motivation and a sequence and process that improves your judgement and effectiveness in whatever sphere of life you choose to apply it to.

In our research for this book, perhaps the greatest failing we encountered has been people's capacity to understand one another, to see the world through another's eyes. As you may have surmised from the title, what this means is that we are all just a little too selfish, scared and stupid to notice that so too is everyone else. Consequently, the world suffers from poor communication, fractured connections and little engagement. Instead, we all bleat on about ourselves and then complain that no one is listening.

But why does this quest to understand human behaviour matter so much?

WHO THIS BOOK IS FOR

Truthfully, we are all behavioural researchers and strategists. It starts at birth and it is a skill we develop and refine throughout our lives. Every child who dominates their parents' attention, every attractive man or woman who uses their physical beauty to their advantage and every rebel who captures the imagination with their charisma is an expert manipulator and behavioural strategist. However, even though there are some supremely gifted practitioners of this art, few have mastered this skill, which informs virtually every decision we make.

Clearly, this is a book about business applications in leadership, sales, human resources, training and motivation; however, it also informs all the areas of our lives where we want to increase our influence and enthusiasm. Human behaviour and motivation also affects how we educate; how we support our children; the achievement of our goals; and our ability to play a larger role in our communities, drive change at a political level or simply increase our capacity to engage those around us socially.

There is no doubt that the central premise of this book is a challenging one—few of us like to think of ourselves as selfish, scared or stupid. Indeed, for decades, self-help and self-management tomes have argued to the contrary, blowing smoke up our collective backsides, seducing us with the messages we've secretly longed to hear, such as, 'You are magnificent, unique and a bundle of pure potentiality'. Their extraordinary and often unsubstantiated theories enable us to drink the Kool-Aid, editorialise our behaviour and turn a blind eye to the reality that we are perhaps not as 'pure' of intent as we may like to think.

However, what we hope to offer our readers is a level of freedom from the restrictions of the past via a more open embracing of the things that make us human, as well as some strategies and tools to make our very same humanity an asset that helps us be more effective leaders, more persuasive salespeople, more respected parents and much more satisfied with the results that we produce in our lives.

But first, we have to admit that we are all selfish, scared and stupid...

PART I

We are all selfish, scared and stupid

Please, don't be offended by this heading. As you will learn, we owe rather a lot to being selfish, scared and stupid. In fact, these qualities are not to be shunned but rather understood and even applauded.

A matter of survival
Being selfish, scared and stupid has shaped our evolution and helped us rise to the top of the food chain despite other species having better strength, speed, more acute senses and even, occasionally, more cunning.

The Happy Delusion
We delude ourselves about what really drives our behaviour and how this can cost us success, effectiveness and a connection with reality—but why?

Why failure happens
We have structured our systems, processes, organisations and entire communities in such a way that we fight our human nature and instead expect laboratory-like consistency in the real world.

CHAPTER 1

A matter of survival

Extinction is the rule. Survival is the exception.

Carl Sagan

Congratulations. If you are reading this book, you have descended from a proud line of selfish, scared and stupid people. Those who came before you managed to look after themselves long enough to reproduce, although back in the days when your forebears wandered the earth, this was not what we would now consider a ripe old age. In fact, back then the age of reproduction was a great deal lower, an age that most cultures today would likely consider a 'land yourself in jail' age.

However, it is still a feat worth acknowledging as so many generations before us failed to pass on their genetic material to our current generation. If they had not been such a selfish, scared and stupid (not to mention horny) lot, you would not be reading the book currently resting in your hands (or on your tablet, if that is your preferred medium).

In fact, your line would most likely have been erased from history in an act of over-complicated bravery or selflessness that perhaps involved a cave, a large ferocious animal or a strange-looking plant and an overly curious palate. And so, this is rather a strange book in that it begins with a happy ending—your arrival at this point in history—bravo!

Charles Darwin is often described as the first proponent of the idea of survival of the fittest. Many of us presume it was Darwin who coined the phrase, but it was actually British polymath philosopher Herbert Spencer who, as part of an impressive résumé, lays claim to this honour (although it must be pointed out that this was achieved only after reading Darwin's *On the Origin of Species*).

In modern usage, the phrase is taken in a context that is perhaps at odds with its original meaning, but let's suppose the widely (mis)-understood context is correct and it simply denotes that 'the strongest and most dominant survive'. At this point it seems worth reminding our readers that human beings were far from the strongest species on the planet. Nor were we the fittest.

In fact, humanity survived and thrived principally because we were acutely aware of our frailties. We lived in a world where we were in constant danger and it is this that forced us to work hard at compensating for our weaknesses and doing whatever it took to keep ourselves breathing and breeding.

And so, we improvised, we invented; we adapted; we looked for ways of protecting ourselves; and we laid low when we needed to. Perhaps 'survival of the fittest' would be more reflective of our evolution if it were phrased thus: 'survival of the most uncomplicated, terrified and self-interested'.

Now, before you begin to take offence at what some may call a disparaging description of our shared origins, take a moment to consider just how successful a strategy it has been. Which other species has been selfish, scared and stupid enough to conceive of sending another species into a mine in its stead to test whether the air is safe to breathe? Or wary enough to persuade another of its own kind to test its food for fear of poisoning? 'Praegustators', as the Romans referred to them, are a uniquely human invention (not an entirely foolproof plan as, in ancient Rome, the praegustator to the emperor Claudius failed to detect the supposed poisoned mushrooms that are widely believed to have ultimately sealed his fate). Adolf Hitler was also renowned to have been so acutely paranoid about his food being poisoned that he didn't just have one food taster—he forced 15 women to taste his food before he ate it. Even in today's White House, the president of the United States is believed to have a food taster of sorts, although naturally the White House will neither confirm nor deny the rumour. Leaving aside the moral repercussions of this practice, you still have to admire the ingenuity and creativity a little selfishness and fear provides.

These survival strategies have been highly useful. Human beings have managed to overcome species and dangers that were larger and far more dangerous than ourselves. We have survived countless natural threats and endured famines, diseases and disasters. We have lived and even thrived in hostile environments with no fur, fangs, poison or claws to speak of. Of course, there may have been a few million or so casualties along the way, but you can't make an omelette without breaking a few eggs now, can you?

Survival is a feat thousands of other species failed to achieve. In fact, scientists estimate that the success of the human species has accelerated what is considered to be a natural rate of extinction by 1000 to 10000 times. Judging by those numbers, we did not simply survive—we conquered, becoming the dominant species on the planet. Although, in retrospect, this domination may come to be our ultimate undoing as we push this planet to the brink of perhaps our own extinction.

The members of our herd who were strategic enough—or rather selfish, scared and stupid enough—to survive and rise through the ranks of the food chain were not the brave, selfless souls who engineered complicated solutions and stood fearlessly to face impending storms or rampaging armies, or who nursed people in times of famine and disease. No, they were far more likely to be the ones bunkering down in the storm, standing well behind the battle lines and keeping conspicuously to themselves in times of viral epidemics.

So, given our cultural biases to celebrate the generous, brave and intellectual, how is it that being selfish, scared and stupid was not only an asset to our ancestors, but remains an asset to those of us who live in the modern world?

SELFLESSNESS IS A RECIPE FOR EXTINCTION

Nursing the sick is one of those moments moviemakers love to employ to reassure us of the power of hope, faith, love and belief. We've all seen the moment on screen, stirring strings that slowly swell as a lone tear trickles down a pale cheek. A sleepless night. A fever. Despair. You think all is lost until... the music stills. A finger moves and then... a breath. Joy. Relief. Love at first bleary sight. Most certainly, those keeping vigil at the bedside of a stranger may be generous, noble and selfless, but in times of epidemic and rampant disease, it's hardly the most effective survival strategy.

Let's be frank, the best approach for survival in these circumstances involves selfishness, quarantine and a vast distance, preferably over a large body of water or an impenetrable mountain range.

Throughout history, being selfless has often meant extinction. Consider the ultimate expression of selflessness: the martyr. Whether they be religious or political zealots they all have a few things in common: putting themselves last, an unwavering belief and a family tree that looks like it has had a rather too severe pruning.

Much of our success as a species is due to our innate pull to protect our lives and those of our loved ones first and foremost. It is not in our still very primal natures to act in a selfless way towards strangers or other species that may threaten our own wellbeing (or else contribute to our diet).

This is one of the problems faced by charities. Their primary communications largely revolve around persuading the rest of us to look after a poor, unfortunate soul who has nothing at all to do with our own wellbeing. Though heartfelt and inspiring, it is a message that goes against thousands of years of hard wiring.

It should come as no surprise then, that organisations that try to enlist our help by garnering a sympathy vote, or confronting us with images designed to make us feel guilt or pity for complete strangers, are often more likely to elicit a desire to change the channel, or flip or click through to the next page.

People tend to think of charities as largely kind and benevolent organisations, driven by the need to serve the greater good. And this is mostly true, at least at the level of conscious intention until, of course, it comes to competing with other good causes for limited support and attention.

There are more than 2 million registered charities in the US, more than 1.7 million in the UK and more than 60000 in Australia, with numbers growing rapidly. The world of charities is as competitive as *The Hunger Games* and the generosity of people finite. It is a jungle out there and to get through it, you need a machete. As callous as this probably sounds, there is only so much open generosity available to provide the help or headspace these worthy causes need.

While it may sound oddly contradictory, charities need to Think Selfish. Instead of starting from a position of, 'Who are the people they wish to help?', a more effective strategy may be to start with why the people they want to engage would *want* to help. In other words, understanding what drives human beings to give in the first place.

People 'give' to charities for all sorts of reasons, but when we truly boil it down, at some point we realise that giving actually makes us feel good. There is a reward of sorts on both sides of the equation. So while we like to think of giving to charity as … well … an act of charity, at some level we're probably doing it to make ourselves feel good (or occasionally because we're scared of what will happen to us spiritually if we don't help out our fellow human beings).

We all like to think of ourselves as good people. For instance, no-one answers a questionnaire by saying, 'I am a bad person at heart', nor do they tend to describe themselves as self-focused or say they rank the rest of humanity on a scale that has themselves and their families comfortably situated at the top in positions that are not open to anything remotely similar to democracy or debate. This, in fact, is one of the limitations of unsophisticated research that fails to filter answers for underlying truths.

Research groups are often asked questions such as, 'Do you consider yourself open minded?' No-one ever says, 'Well, no. You know what, I am utterly closed minded, painfully stuck in my ways with an unwavering inability to see any point of view but my own'. We are all far more likely to say, 'Yes, yes, of course I am'.

We all like to feel as though we are not painfully prejudiced and loyal to our own opinions over those of others. We all want to feel good about who looks back at us in the mirror each morning. We are socialised to believe that self-sacrifice and a charitable nature are virtues to be proud of, and often they are.

However, today most charities have begun to understand what makes us tick and they are moving into the retail industry. Once upon a time we were asked to give money to show our support. Today we are asked to buy something: from ribbons of every colour imaginable, to red noses, T-shirts, bears wrapped in bandages and flowers; and every Movember or Muffvember, men around the world are even asked to pay for the pleasure of growing a moustache, while women pay for the privilege of not tidying up downstairs (without putting too fine a point on it).

Marketeers working within charities now realise that merchandising, with its inherent gain, is more appealing than simply parting with cash. The important question this trend raises is, 'Why?' Why is a red ribbon more appealing than a heart-wrenching plea from an AIDS sufferer in a hospital bed?

Throughout this book, we'll assert that it is because one approach asks us to be generous without any sense of personal gain, while the other not only gives us something physical in return, it gives us something intangible too, something that shows the world who we are and confers upon us social status and currency.

In other words, Thinking Selfish is still a vital strategy for survival, success and, ultimately, generosity.

SELFISH IS HARD TO RESIST

Self-interest drives us more than most of us would care to admit. Consider something as mundane and everyday as the wave you hope you get when you let another driver pull in front of you in a line of traffic. We all long for the wave; we look for the wave and we get surprisingly irritated or even irate if we fail to receive one.

We once shared a stage with a Buddhist monk when the topic of lack of gratitude came up. 'People are so ungrateful, even when you do something generous like letting them into traffic', someone in the room lamented.

The wise old monk smiled in a knowing way, paused thoughtfully and then asked, 'Why did you let them in, in the first place?'

The person indignantly replied, 'to do something nice for someone else'.

The monk questioned further. 'Are you certain?'

'Yes,' the person protested, 'it was a kind thing to do'.

The monk calmly observed that, 'perhaps you did it because you wanted to be acknowledged. You wanted that feeling that comes from being nice to someone else'.

Of course, it is quite hard to argue against this logic as, upon reflection, we may all question the total purity of our 'kinder' motives.

This same line of thinking underpins why throughout Asia, monks often do not acknowledge gifts of food or assistance. As they see it, people are essentially buying good karma by taking care of the holy men. They see it not as a generous act, rather as a selfish one: the sense of satisfaction that we get; the self-righteous feeling that enables us to think of ourselves as decent human beings; and the hope that we'll get an upgrade to first class when our number ultimately comes up.

This explains why monks often do not bow or verbally thank the people who support them. They understand that even when we think we are being kind, we are often driven by our own selfish needs.

Of course, we are not monks and while we are making a case to Think Selfish, a thank you and a wave are still welcome responses.

FEARLESSNESS LEADS TO EXTINCTION

Being fearless can lead to extinction. The famously extinct dodo bird was reputedly fearless. When confronted with a strange new species, did it run? Hide? Or fight? No, it stood bravely and trustingly. (To be fair, the fact that the species couldn't fly did not help the situation. But surely if you have a trusting nature and can't fly, you at least learn to walk rather quickly.)

Acts of fearlessness often don't end well. There is a reason we instinctively feel fear around spiders and snakes and even of the dark. Quite simply, these things can harm us, often fatally. Imagine what it was like to wander into a dark cave in prehistoric times. Cold, tired and hungry (not to mention disgustingly pungent), all you want to do is get out of the elements and find a place to sleep, so you bravely step up to the threshold and cross into the unknown.

Unfortunately, you are not the only creature to have that thought on this particular evening. And, as it turns out, the other creature is equipped with immense size, brute strength, a sense of smell that is virtually a super power, claws, possibly venom ... oh, and it also has the kind of night vision only navy SEALs are supposed to have.

The work of Walter Bradford Cannon posits that we face two possible responses in this dark-cave scenario: 'fight or flight'. Our bodies instinctively react in seconds to prepare us for either option. The hypothalamus triggers and our adrenal glands also kick in.

Now, although fight is an option, it does not take much of an imagination to realise flight may be the preferable survival strategy in this scenario. Besides, it is dark and no-one will see us take the coward's way out.

The moral to the story—unlike the dangerously unrealistic 'Little Red Riding Hood' scenario—is that we should be afraid of the big bad wolf. The big bad wolf will likely kill or maim you nine times out of 10. And if we're honest, an old man wandering around the woods with an axe is equally deserving of suspicion and hardly someone we should count on in a pinch.

Our most common natural phobias—and this should be seen as no coincidence—tend to be linked to the potentially fatal, or at least the highly damaging. Snakes, spiders, heights, water, bugs and death are among the most common human fears, and for very good reason: they present us with mortal danger.

In our evolution, fearlessness, though much admired, was a recipe for having stories told about us in the past tense. Fearlessness usually doesn't have a happy ending because the fearless, more often than not, did not live happily ever after.

FEAR: ONE OF THE MOST MOTIVATING EMOTIONS WE POSSESS

Fear, it transpires, is perhaps more moving than inspiration, love and a month-long Anthony Robbins audio series. It even drives sales of products worth billions of dollars.

We fear death; we fear failure; we fear rejection; we fear the unknown; and we fear getting older. We are terrified of wrinkles, body odour, too much hair or the lack thereof (depending on the body part we're talking about), flatulence, halitosis, impotence, the wrong-coloured shoes and our children not keeping up with those around them. All around the planet industries thrive and grow in proportion to our scaredy-cat natures. An enormous proportion of the dollars we spend are fuelled by our fear: beauty, defence, self-help, anti-ageing (which isn't even technically possible), health, weight loss, fashion and insurance to name a few.

A friend of ours posted a rather insightful meme to Facebook that said, 'What if the women of the world woke up and decided they liked their bodies? Entire industries would go out of business'. A rather sad but poignant observation.

In a study from McCann Worldgroup, a global advertising agency, mothers all around the world were asked what they wanted most for their children. Perhaps unsurprisingly, happiness was the most common answer. The exception was in India. In India, mothers still harboured a greater desire for success and wealth (so if your mother is Indian, sorry: you will have to study and become a doctor).

Some people were surprised, almost horrified, that a mother should value wealth and success over happiness as if it were written in the Mother Handbook that 'Thou shalt put thy child's happiness above all else'.

But consider where India is in its economic development. It is a nation with an ever-widening gap between rich and poor. Simply maintaining survival is still an issue. Success and wealth in a country still trying to overcome extreme poverty are likely to seem far more important than the rewards offered by rungs higher up Maslow's hierarchy of needs. In this environment, success and wealth are also likely to be considered critical markers on the way to achieving this eventual happiness. The truth is, it is only in nations where basic needs are amply covered that mothers have the luxury of prioritising their children's happiness.

Ironically, the more of this wealth and 'happiness' we achieve, the more fear begins to drive and motivate us as not only do we fear for our survival, but we begin to fear loss as well.

COMPLICATION AND COMPLEXITY LEAD TO EXTINCTION

A capacity to comprehend the complicated and to interact with complexity, a bias towards hard-earned achievement and an all-round smarty-pantsness, while annoying, are generally considered to be a demonstration of what life is like for successful human beings.

However, throughout our evolution it is these very things that have consistently gotten in the way of our survival and have in fact counted against us as weaknesses.

For our purposes throughout this book, when we advocate for Thinking Stupid, what we are actually referring to is our natural tendency to like things to be simple, easy and if at all possible, low involvement. In other words, stupidly simple and easy (read lazy).

Despite its potential to leave us exhausted, possibly injured, confused or even dead, we tend to believe that hard work ultimately pays off and that complexity is essential for keeping ahead of the pack. But this is not always the case. Whoever said 'hard work never killed anyone' was more than a little off the mark.

The great undertakings of humanity did not come without cost, and we don't mean simply fiscal. Many of the spectacularly ambitious endeavours of humankind—including the Egyptian pyramids, the expansion of virtually every empire and kingdom, monuments, grand railways, river explorations, mines of every description and mineral output, dams and even the space race—required hard work, complicated risk and an enormous cost to human life.

During its construction, the Great Wall of China was frequently referred to as 'the largest cemetery on earth' due to the incredible loss of life that came with this extraordinary undertaking. It is believed that approximately one million people lost their lives while it was being built. So hard work has actually killed an enormous number of people.

Being a hard working or diligent student is not always a recipe for popularity and can even turn you into a victim of bullying.

But it is not just the smart kids who have targets on them. Throughout our history great empires and leaders have fallen prey to being too clever by half and leading anything but simple, easy lives. So much so that famous idioms were spawned as warnings to us all: 'Pride comes before a fall' and every mother's favourite, 'You're gettin' a bit too big for your boots'.

Thinking Stupid, however, likes to keep things easy; it finds the simplest way of doing things. It uses fewer and shorter words to communicate meaning or even visuals to share critical warnings succinctly. Thinking Stupid is also lazy, so if there is a shortcut Stupid will find it. In doing so, it enables us to avoid over-thinking or over-complicating things, confusion, notions of superiority and time-wasting. These very features are the ones that helped us survive and yet we ignore them and in fact deride them.

But if we take the time to learn to Think Stupid, it will serve our survival. Stupid drives us forward

Necessity isn't the mother of all invention: laziness is. If it is hard or complex, or simply unwieldy, human beings will mostly avoid it or look for another way.

The invention of the wheel, the development of agriculture, the telegraph, refrigeration, home delivery, drive-through shopping, the internet: they all evolved out of a desire to make life simpler and easier, and to create less work.

A plethora of new inventions, innovations and life improvements has emerged over the years to help our lives seem simpler, less labour intensive and less taxing on the thinking front. In this, being Stupid has in fact driven us to be smarter, not in the cognitive sense of the word, but in a more street-smart manner.

Take one of the essential elements for sustaining life: water. We all understand that water is essential, but let's be honest, that river is just too darn far away. Hello plumbing! Today we're all very happy with our plumbing and few of us relish the thought of going back to nature every time nature calls.

Thinking Stupid makes us efficient and direct, and it promotes clarity and simplicity — skills and characteristics critical not just for survival but also for success in the modern world.

DON'T FIGHT YOUR NATURE: WORK WITH IT

Though it has served us well over the millennia, we still fight our nature and deny our selfish, scared and stupid roots, not because they no longer serve us, but because we have created social constructs against them in our communities, our industries and even in our families.

We spend most of our lives trying to force our behaviours to fit social expectations, guilt-tripping ourselves into generosity, pushing ourselves to be brave and berating ourselves as stupid and lazy for simply feeling a natural emotion.

This, as we will argue, is a mistake. Not only does it rob us of our natural motivation and instinct, it forces us to adopt behaviours that, though widely applauded, are not in fact successful a lot of the time.

Selfish offers us a connection to what truly matters to us and a guard against value systems being imposed upon us. It teaches us to look out for our own interests and drives us towards personal success. Scared makes us wary and savvy, and helps us assert control over a world where out-of-control is the norm. Stupid fuels our creativity, makes us resourceful and drives our communications and systems to become simpler, easy to understand and foolproof.

These factors are much more than the tools of human survival; they are the critical elements we need to understand in order to drive engagement, innovation and success in ourselves, our organisations, our communities and in those around us. But they oblige us to be willing to lose the scales from our eyes and to see through the delusions we've been taught to believe in.

CHAPTER 2

The Happy Delusion

The trouble with giving yourself a pep talk is, that
deep down you know it's all bullshit.

Sophie Kinsella

Despite our survival being inextricably linked to our basest thoughts and desires, we don't like to think of ourselves as being quite so simple, or indeed base. In fact, complexity is seen as a state so desirable that entire subcultures, such as goths, emos and corporate MBAs, devote themselves to its worship, each choosing to hide behind the passive-aggressive mantra of, 'You just wouldn't understand...'

Of course, while some aspects of life, business and personal development do raise complicated questions and conflicts that must be dealt with using the more energy-consuming regions of our brains, the problem is, we come to see this as our default rather than as an anomaly or exception to the rule.

Society too reinforces the belief that life is less simple than we may secretly long for it to be and, oddly enough, we actually find comfort in this complexity. After all, how could we possibly be expected to 'get it together' when it's all so dreadfully difficult? And so we begin to accept this 'devil we know' and its accompanying learnt helplessness, choosing instead to blame ourselves and the abilities of those around us rather than the strategies we have enlisted to navigate our lives.

What this is really about is a cover-up of a less than glamorous truth and our indulgence in The Happy Delusion.

WHAT IS THE HAPPY DELUSION?

The Happy Delusion informs our behaviour in every aspect of our lives. It leads us to focus only on the positive results we see around us and to ignore anything we deem to be negative, such as failure, cruel thoughts, personal upsets and disappointing (though insight-filled) feedback.

This delusion also becomes important to human beings as we traverse the various social roles we transition through in the course of our lives, from child to student to employee to parent to leader. Each of these roles either lends support to the delusion, sustaining its growth and development, or else benefits us as we align with the social expectations of others who share it.

The Happy Delusion works at a number of different levels. First, it demonises some rather natural human responses and emotions. It states that stress and fear are always bad, posits that selfishness is a thought crime to be banished from 'more-evolved' minds, that being lazy is wasteful and that shortcuts are the road to ruin and will ultimately compromise both quality and fulfilment.

What is perhaps more dangerous is that it also makes a rather strong case for a belief to the contrary. It asserts that being a workaholic should be lauded; self-sacrifice should be praised; and bravery to the point of absurd personal risk should be respected in spite of the very real potential cost to life, limb and property. Unsurprisingly, many — if not most — of our 'heroes' have died some pretty grizzly deaths.

HOW DOES THIS DELUSION FORM?

So, how is it that we choose to embrace falsehood when navigating our way through life? How does falsehood spread so effectively and why is it so seldom challenged?

Consider for a moment how we arrive in this world: Is there anything quite so exquisitely self-obsessed as a newborn baby? Consumed with their own need for survival they completely dominate conversation, attention and resources. Children seem to challenge our concept of a heliocentric solar system, suggesting instead a me-centric model (a description that also describes much of the behaviour of the first world in our less-than-charitable moments).

In our infancy we are driven by the desire to satisfy our hunger as well as the need to find refuge and security in the arms of those we depend on, and to keep our desires simple and to the point: eat … poop … sleep … repeat! This single-mindedness is essential to our survival, and those who (tragically) find themselves denied this introduction to life, often sadly don't survive.

And yet, from the moment we are born a process begins whereby we are encouraged to curb our personal desires. We are socialised to believe that denying our own personal biases and desires in favour of feigned generosity, displays of reckless courage and the acceptance of dizzying complexity is not only preferable, but superior. Of course, it must be said that these skills do aid us in our development as social beings. Certainly, acting like a toddler whenever we fail to get our way is often a recipe for disaster (or, quite possibly, a career in politics).

But the delusion goes deeper than this. It is not that we simply adopt new skills as we grow up; we also learn to ignore, and even revile, the characteristics that allowed us the privilege of growing up in the first place; that is, the selfish, scared and stupid characteristics. These deep desires still sit at the root of our character, but we take great pride in banishing them to the recesses of our minds and revelling in our 'higher' values, seeing ourselves as good people who twinge with guilt whenever this thin veneer is scratched.

As a result, many of us live within limits that we no longer even see, let alone question. We accept this view of reality as reality itself and reconcile selfish, survival-focused thinking as a vestige of our foolish youth.

Schools, social conventions and the organisations we interact with assist us in the delusion as, all around the world, people are instructed to 'focus on the positive', to 'ignore the negative', to 'be generous and brave' and to 'play to our strengths'.

This strategy for success seems to make logical sense: if you're good at something, why wouldn't you focus on it and do more of it? After all, as you become expert at something, you tend to enjoy it more, and you receive more positive feedback from your peers and superiors, as well as gaining a greater sense of self-satisfaction. And so, this seemingly virtuous circle continues.

However, as most professional athletes and other high achievers can attest, it is in working on our weaknesses that we truly begin to lift our entire game. In fact, one of the pitfalls of choosing to play only to our strengths is that our strengths are typically category generic. In other words, in a room filled with carpenters, being good with a hammer is a rather less than impressive skill.

Putting logic aside for a moment, the real reason our Happy Delusion is so resilient is that it just feels right. It feels good. Who wouldn't, given the choice, want their experience of life to be more characterised by only positive reinforcement, with all of the negatives swept neatly under the rug. Interestingly, this desire in itself hints at our underlying selfishness.

This line of thinking is echoed in the sentiment often expressed by sanctimonious types who claim to have very simple desires. These 'simple' souls are regularly heard to exclaim, 'I just want to be happy'. Let's be clear, it is only the inclusion of the word 'just' that makes this statement seem so reasonable and small when in fact it is anything but. The desire to 'just be happy' suggests that one's life is completely out of balance, with absolutely no downside and supporting a constant experience of bliss and encouragement—hardly a small or reasonable request at all.

But it's not just that we've been duped by society; we also delude ourselves. We are encouraged to change ourselves to fit with an idealised system, rather than building a system that fits with our present reality, and the truth is, that suits most of us just fine.

One of the reasons why The Happy Delusion is so powerful is that we learn to internalise it as inner dialogue. And so, the deluded become the delusion. This occurs because most of us, if we're honest, like to think of ourselves as good people and these are the values we tend to associate with goodness. The truth is, we often *are* good people ... just not precisely in the way we think we are.

This is where the break with reality really begins to pick up momentum.

Very early on, we learn to edit reality to fit with our conception of ourselves. We tend to see the world not as it is, but as we are. In other words, we filter reality looking for those 'facts' that best fit with our world-view. The way we view reality works very much in line with the Reticular Activating System (RAS). The RAS is most often explained using the parable of the person who buys a new car then begins to see the same model of car almost everywhere. In the same way, we also notice the things in our world that confirm rather than challenge the way we see things.

What this means is that our information-gathering senses are not particularly open-minded or indeed accurate; in other words, we lie to ourselves in an effort to stay happy and congruent, which is an extremely powerful motivator.

One of the most fascinating series of psychological experiments of recent times explores this theme more deeply. In these studies, subjects are asked to recall details of a recent experience; for example, they may be asked to provide a visual description of the participants of a particular event that was staged for them to witness. Although this seems like a simple enough task, in many cases the subjects' descriptions of the participants varied so wildly from reality as to be truly shocking.

What this research uncovered was that rather than simply accessing memories, the participants' descriptions of the event had to first pass through their own filters and prejudices. This, of course, distorted the reality they described. The results of these types of studies are often cited as criticism of eyewitness statements as reliable testimony during trials, but for our purposes, they simply serve to illustrate how our information-gathering is often coloured by our pre-formed world-view.

This psychological predisposition means The Happy Delusion is not only likely to be maintained, but is also incredibly hard to shift. How do you remove or change something you can no longer see or even perceive?

In fact, it is not unreasonable to assert that human beings seldom truly understand what really drives them at all, nor the teams in their charge, their customers, constituents or even the communities they live in.

This means that when we deny the parts of ourselves that we don't like — or, perhaps more accurately, those we have been socialised to cover up and repress as a way of fitting in — we begin to experience conflict with reality and this can get us into rather a lot of bother.

It seems, despite any Tom Cruise–like proclamations, that we 'want the truth' in our lives; we actually quite like the delusion. Not only does it make us feel good and seem to be good, it makes us look good too … and that is a powerful stimulant when it comes to human behaviour.

THE QUALITIES OF THE MYTHICAL HERO

Being generous, bold and intelligent fits with our idealised values of what a human being of unshakeable character should embody. These are the values different cultures have for millennia held up as desirable and as a noble example for others to follow.

Throughout history we have sanitised our myths and editorialised the exploits of those we admire. Our so-called 'real-life' heroes are most often praised for their discipline, bravery, wisdom and nobility, while the reality of their actions are carefully glossed over. This suggests we create a distorted picture of what it means to succeed and a false path for others to follow.

The tendency has been to revere and reinvent extraordinary human beings such as Mahatma Gandhi and Nelson Mandela after their deaths. Both of these men, judging by their own written work, were well aware of their own personal failings as well as what it had taken for them to achieve their professional and political success and to drive the social change they realised in their very human lifetimes.

Likewise, in the generations prior to live battle-cams and whistle-blowing websites, war crimes were seen as atrocities only committed by 'the other side', or more accurately, something only the losing nation was capable of. As a result, although most of society's heroes are undoubtedly deserving, or at least very successful, our view of how they came to achieve their heroic status is mostly incomplete and often inaccurate.

This delusion not only informs what is considered ideal in an individual, it also shapes the opinions and beliefs of how society, our communities, large corporations, our governments, leaders, laws, processes and systems should be organised. This is largely because The Happy Delusion helps us feel in control. If we believe that we as individuals are mostly driven by our better angels, and that those around us also seem to be, then the world appears safer and more predictable. It is interesting to note that most people who publicly decry any infringement on their own personal liberties are often the most annoying sticklers when it comes to everyone else obeying the rules. Control, it seems, is the name of the game.

And so, in our social and business interactions we operate within a silent covenant among those we share our lives with. This unspoken contract best translates as, 'If you don't challenge my delusion I won't challenge yours'. We try very carefully to monitor our behaviour, to never truly say what's on our minds or reveal what's really important to us for fear of being discovered. Instead, we put on a facade of faux-politeness, indulging in political correctness and sublimating our anger and self-loathing. We try to appear in control and commanding, doing our best to hide any hint of weakness or ignorance and only express our true feelings when we reach breaking point (at which point we typically unload our emotional baggage on those who least deserve it).

BUT IT *IS* A DELUSION AND DELUSIONS COST US

Delusions cost us in our businesses and in our relationships principally because we are being informed by ideals, not realities. They cost us at a cultural level too as we adopt belief systems that don't match up with what we know to be true and how we typically behave. And our delusions also have a detrimental effect at a societal level. If we want to do good and expect others to do good, we need to first admit that we are mostly inclined not to do a great deal of good without a good reason.

This is one of the principal reasons why social movements struggle to gain traction and the funds they often desperately require. Those who are personally invested in an issue — be it through personal or familial experience or through being enrolled by a charismatic leader — tend to believe that others should be likewise invested in the cause based only on its own merits.

Sadly, this often doesn't translate to the engagement they desire and leaves them blaming other people as selfish (which of course they are, if only in that they consider something personal to *their* experience to be more worthy). Instead of feeling frustrated, underperforming in terms of their leadership, or blaming others or even themselves, a better strategy would be to engage people in a realistic and far more successful way — in other words, to anchor their cause in the values system of those they seek to persuade: 'If you want me to care about what's important to you, link it to what's important to me'.

Perhaps most concerning though, is that the delusion costs us personally. Most of us harbour a genuine desire to do the right thing, and yet this desire sets us up for failure because we fail to acknowledge what's really driving us at our core. Instead, we try to force our behaviour to live up to externalised value systems enlisting blunt tools such as discipline and denial.

Ultimately, we fail because we do not like to even consider failure, whereas success accepts that failure is part of the process and accounts for it accordingly.

The Happy Delusion manifests in our lives like so many other delusions. It is the sum total of smaller deceits that we buy into. It exists in the little lies we tell ourselves daily and in the folksy homilies we accept without ever questioning their veracity. Here are 10 to be aware of.

Stress and fear are bad

Very few of us actually enjoy feelings of stress and fear, but not only are they entirely natural emotional responses to different stimuli, they are also rather useful when it comes to navigating treacherous environments; that is, those environments that have the potential to present us with physical or intellectual harm. Of course, these emotions can over-index in our experience and cloud our better judgement, but is this because these emotions are intrinsically wrong or because the way we process them is incorrect?

Despite their usefulness, doctors, naturopaths and therapists are constantly lecturing us to lower our stress levels, while self-help gurus encourage us to ignore, minimise and defeat our fears. However, experts such as health psychologist and TEDster Kelly McGonigal have revealed that research challenges this view.

In her 2013 TED talk, after admitting to prescribing against stress and fear in the past, she asserts that stress and fear may not necessarily be the cause of the physical and emotional distress attached to them. Rather, McGonigal suggests that this distress, characterised by physical manifestations such as unhealthily raised blood pressure and acute anxiety, is linked not to the stress and fear itself but to the expectation that they shouldn't be a part of our experience at all. In other words, stress and fear are made worse by bad PR, or by the delusion that they shouldn't, in fact, exist.

We should focus only on the positives

Another key tenet of The Happy Delusion is the desire to deny or cover up any negatives and to exaggerate the positives. For instance, when we catch ourselves acting uncharitably, being niggardly or speaking rudely, we tend to process this as a departure from our usual character rather than accepting it as a part of our varied whole as human beings. We are inclined to do the same in social situations, business strategies, personal growth and even in leadership roles.

Of course, the problem with such strategies is that they don't work. In fact, ignoring the negatives and exaggerating the positives can often have us writing cheques our bodies (or minds or teams) can't cash. This misreading, or misrepresentation, of reality means that being overly positive too often leads to negative results.

Heroes are successful by good deeds alone

As already alluded to, when it comes to stories about our heroes, even those who are non-fiction, we tend towards myth and legend. This is not to say that we disrespect the reality of those who have achieved great things, but rather that we tend to ignore anything they did that doesn't fit with the heroism of what they achieved.

We mentioned Nelson Mandela earlier who, along with his supporters, helped to right one of the greatest social injustices of our time. Along the way, however, he encouraged civil disobedience, broke any number of laws he decided he didn't agree with and has gone on record admitting to planning and executing bombings of unmanned bridges and South African government sites.

All of this helped him build the foundation for what was to come and was an unpleasant necessity for creating both an impetus for change and international engagement in a cause that had been largely ignored. And yet, he is painted only as a man of peace who achieved his success by peaceful protest.

So why should this 'cleaning up of the details' matter so much? It matters because if we are to follow Mandela's example, we must first understand the completeness of the example. In other words, what did his success truly require and are we equally prepared to pay this price?

We operate rationally and morally

Despite its increasing trajectory towards the secular, human culture quite likes to hold onto the belief that we mostly operate in alignment with a higher moral compass. However, most of our laws and even our community ethics are transitory and have changed and morphed over the centuries as culture and belief systems have shifted.

Making these changes 'stick' has required, variously, military intervention, coercion, physical force, police patrols, fines, the threat of imprisonment, hostage taking and the Spanish Inquisition.

So if you think we're well behaved simply because we're rational and moral, think again.

It will all work out in the end

This is the grown-up equivalent of pulling the blankets up over our heads and hoping that the bogeyman goes away. The primary issue with this strategy, aside from its obvious childishness, is that it relies on hope rather than action to change our circumstances—a strategy that is, at best, a fifty-fifty option.

The most important good is looking good

As already asserted, The Happy Delusion not only makes us feel good, it makes us look good. To a greater or lesser extent, we all like to indulge in a little social conformity, to not stand out for all the wrong reasons. This little deceit, the changing of who we actually are in order to retain a measure of popularity, is perhaps the most insidious of the lies we tell ourselves, as it seems so reasonable and pays to us what we often feel are huge dividends. But, in the end, it also costs us who we truly are and removes our connection with reality.

Ignore your critics and detractors

The mantra of ignoring our detractors has almost become part of the self-help canon. We have been counselled to not listen to the nay-sayers even if they live in our head, to ignore the experts if their advice runs counter to our dream, and to spurn critics lest they become obstacles in our way. And it is easy to see why this thinking has become so popular.

The truth is, the deceit we discussed previously—our compulsion to 'look good'—does in many cases have us paying too much attention to those who are not necessarily expert in the case at hand or who have no real connection to our personal circumstances.

The problem is, our critics often have just as much chance of being right as we do. Certainly, we shouldn't abdicate our decision-making to those who oppose us, but to ignore them and not learn from them is to miss a trick.

One of the questions we often ask businesses we speak to is, 'Who here follows their competitors on Twitter?' The response is typically a little underwhelming: we consider one raised hand a win. Often, a brave heckler will call out, 'We run our own race. We don't worry about what the competition is up to', to which we respond, 'Yes, but do you care what their customers are complaining about?' And then, of course, the penny drops.

So you can see that our critics are not there to provide us with judgement, but rather to test and improve our judgement. Ignoring them costs us another connection with reality.

The universe is conspiring to help you

This statement is a favourite of those who like to dress in unbleached cotton, light incense in their inner-city apartments and grow hair in socially challenging regions of their bodies. In other words, people who like to drink the Kool-Aid.

Of course, it is often used as a counter to the cry of the victim, 'The universe hates me'. Neither, of course, is true. Given the scale of the universe, it speaks more to delusions of grandeur and significance than anything approaching a scientific understanding of the universe.

The truth is, the universe is otherwise occupied and is neither against us nor on our side. Of course, some reassurance can be taken in the universe's neutrality—if it did in fact hate us we hardly have the resources to fight back—but more than that, ignoring this deceit is an invitation to take greater responsibility for helping ourselves.

Human beings are amazing

The key to any successful lie is to fold in just enough truth to make it seem plausible and the 'human beings are amazing' deceit is an example of how a delusion can be forged using only truths. Human beings are indeed amazing. The complexity and individuality each of us is capable of; the expressions of art and poetry that make our lives all the richer; the acts of generosity that make us blush at the pure intention of the gesture; and the bravery that characterises so much of our history: all of these are truly inspiring.

Of course, what makes these moments so valuable is that they are rare and uncommon. In other words, don't count on them. Even Mozart had an off day where a concerto more likely resembled an oom-pah band on the wrong side of an Oktoberfest beer binge, and it's entirely probable that da Vinci spent an entire week not quite getting the nose right. The point is, although we can be amazing, this is not a strategy we should rely on if we want to achieve consistent results.

Delusion beats reality

'Fake it till you make it'; 'If life gives you lemons, make lemonade'; 'The glass isn't half empty, it's half full'…so many of the folksy homilies that we call 'common sense' seem to speak to disconnecting with reality in favour of delusion. Of course, without squeezing the lemons and adding a whole lot of soluble sugar, you've got some pretty bitter lemonade!

The real issue, however, is that disconnecting from reality robs us of acting in and on our reality. The delusion isn't wrong because it is based on falsehood, it is dangerous because it sets us up for failure.

CHAPTER 3

Why failure happens

Success is not final, failure is not fatal.

Winston Churchill

We live in an era of overindulgence. While the media likes to turn the spotlight on our junk food and computer game–addicted youth, our overindulgence is not confined to the physical (or lack thereof). Today, our psychological lives are also characterised by relentless positivism and happiness delusions as we strive to create a perpetual mono-emotional state, such that we can never be truly sated.

One of the problems with our overindulgence in the positivity and hope fantasies touted by much of the self-help school is that they inform so many of our strategies in business, and in life for that matter. Added to this is the fact that they're not especially helpful if we want to achieve actual results.

Sure they're entertaining and they temporarily make us feel good (self-help's comparison with rock concerts is well earned: you leave on a high, buy the merchandise and a month later it's all gathering dust). But the motivation industry's almost religious status has convinced many of us to abandon our own cognitive processes and 'follow our bliss': trust the universe and invest in a cork-board! (It's important to note at this point that there is a huge distinction between affirmations and mental rehearsal.)

Consequently, great ideas, extraordinary teams, powerful organisations and some exceptionally gifted and talented individuals often fail. This is principally because they haven't even considered the possibility of failure, let alone designed an environment or processes that help them thrive in spite of it.

Worse, they come to blame themselves and process failure as a character trait rather than as simply another result, however undesired it may be.

For instance, if we were to suggest to you that you volunteer to be the test subject for a *never before tested* parachute design that we were really positive and fist-pumpingly confident about, how readily would you give up the option of a reserve chute? The question is almost ridiculous, and yet this formula is repeated in offices, homes, schools and fitness centres around the planet every day. In fact, rather than being the exception, it has become the strategic norm.

We have designed our world in such a way that only perfect execution can succeed ... and just in case you haven't taken a good look around recently, perfection is pretty rare.

Of course, there are a number of reasons for this. It is in our natures to err towards optimism. Hope is quite possibly the most powerful drug we have ever injected into our cerebellums and many of us have an addiction so acute that we will sacrifice almost everything to satisfy it.

Now we're certainly not suggesting that optimism underscored with effort is a bad thing—quite the contrary. What we're talking about is the baseless optimism that dominates so much of our social commentary and leaves us impotent in the face of reality. More importantly, we're asserting that one of the consequences of this kind of optimism is that we court failure by not accounting for it.

We act as if we are generous, bold and intelligent *all the time*, and as a result we adopt hope as a strategy. We shun criticism as pessimism and at the first sign of negativity, we put our fingers in our ears and chant, 'I'm not listening, I'm not listening'. Or else, we double down on a positivity bender and cavort like an evangelical congregation reciting cheery affirmations laced with doubt and desperation: 'I am rich, thin and successful … I am a preciously unique snowflake filled with abundance', and the like.

THE TRUTH IS, WE SET OURSELVES UP FOR FAILURE

Children in modern life are, rather notoriously, never allowed to experience anything remotely like failure (heaven forbid they miss out on a 'pass the parcel' prize). As a result, failure hits them hard when real life refuses to grade them on a curve suspended over a padded floor with a loving acceptance of 'their own special spelling'.

Of course it's easy to pick on children and no-one will thank us for it, so let's turn our attention to the adult world. The same can be said of most corporate and government processes, business systems and self-management programs. The more you set strategy or design systems without a consciousness of even the possibility of failure, the greater the chance of realising that failure actually is.

Diets—or 'wellness programs' as they have come to be euphemised—are famous for simultaneously promising the virtually impossible in record time, and for almost universally failing to provide lasting results. And yet, the more preposterous the claim and the more inflated the possibility, the more these books, powders, audio-programs and reality television shows seem to sell.

What's more concerning is that when we do eventually fail or backslide (the faith-based terminology is not coincidental), we end up blaming ourselves rather than the system we've bought into. We desperately self-flagellate as our internal dialogue runs to phrases such as, 'I'm weak … I'm hopeless … I can't do it …' and so the cycle continues.

By ignoring the possibility of failure in our thinking, we unwittingly increase the chances of it ultimately eventuating.

Contrast this strategy with the design parameters of commercial aircraft. In 2012, while speaking at an international business summit in Bangkok, Thailand, we struck up a conversation with another speaker, Richard de Crespigny. Richard is the Qantas pilot who successfully landed QF32, the Airbus A380 that, en route from Singapore to Sydney, experienced catastrophic engine failure causing an enormous hole in the wing (which, it is pretty well agreed by all flying experts, is rather a bad thing to happen!).

In a typically Australian, self-deprecating way, Richard is quick to deflect credit for the safe arrival away from his skills as a pilot and onto his crew and his aircraft. But when you probe a little deeper into his story, you really do get a sense of just how 'foolproof' the systems built into the A380 actually are.

It turns out that all commercial aircraft are designed with the possibility that they may crash taken into consideration. And this stretches to considerably more than the life vest and its amazing light-and-whistle combination (which no doubt is immensely reassuring as you bob up and down in the middle of a vast ocean). Failure, it turns out, is actually factored into the engineering.

In other words, when a system suffers a serious failure, the plane will, in most cases, stay in the air. It is only in the very unlikely event of multiple system failures of significant magnitude that you may really want to locate the nearest exit (if only to be sure of where holes in the plane are supposed to be).

But even this understates the over-engineering involved in the building of the A380 (given the successful landing of QF32, the term 'over-engineering' may be an overstatement in itself). According to de Crespigny's account, the aircraft exceeded even his expectations and what most pilots would consider its baseline specifications. The plane simply refused to let a ridiculously long string of errors lead to complete failure.

So it appears that, when it comes to things where our lives are at stake (such as sitting in a metal chair at 9000 metres while travelling at 800 kilometres per hour) we start to get a little more realistic about our chances of success and in fact we improve those chances by preparing for the chance of failure.

So how is it that we set ourselves up for failure?

DISCIPLINE IS HARD WORK

As the sun rises on a crisp 1 January morning, those living in the Northern Hemisphere breathe out visible air in the cold as they step into a fresh new world rich with possibilities. Meanwhile those in the Southern Hemisphere, many of whom are already halfway through the new day, bury their toes in the sand on sun-drenched beaches clutching Moleskines and pens with pages optimistically titled 'New Year's Resolutions'.

We may have partied hard over the holiday break but now it is time to get a grip on our lives—to make some 'positive' changes, rein in excesses and do a little exercise, maybe learn a language, be kinder to our livers and perhaps get back to playing the piano.

This is the kind of interior dialogue we all engage in as we usher in a new year (those in Asia no doubt think this is a ridiculous practice best left until the 'real' new year a few weeks later). And what better way to embrace these possibilities than to apply a little healthy discipline. After all, surely that's a good thing. It shows we're willing to take responsibility for our lives and not passively allow life to simply dictate terms to us.

So we swear off alcohol, join a gym, go out and buy some appropriately stretchy fitness attire, throw out every can of soft drink and refill the refrigerator's crisper tray with loads of fresh vegetables (where they will, of course, rot as they have all previous Januaries).

By February, we're berating ourselves, 'Why am I so undisciplined? Why can I not stick to anything? What is wrong with me?'

The answer is, 'Nothing is wrong with you', unless of course you consider being exquisitely human 'wrong'. Yet, much of our culture, certainly the 'self-improvement' industry, asserts that what we are lacking is discipline. They inform us that our attitudes need a tune up, that it's all about our states of mind and that we should push ourselves to higher levels of self-control.

This, of course, is mostly nonsense. Many of those who espouse this herculean discipline, be they personal trainers, life coaches or 'self-actualising consultants', are just as undisciplined in other areas of their own lives. Consider the typical Boot Camp–owning physical trainers who scream at their clients as they torture them in public parks but are incapable of picking their children up from school on time or organising their receipts come tax time. It makes you wonder how they would respond to a rather feeble looking accountant standing over them and screaming, 'You're worthless and weak ... look at your expense reports ... you disgust me!'

Discipline, it seems, owes rather more to the hierarchy of our own personal values and internal filters than it does to any self-imposed directions running to the contrary.

But does that mean we should all surrender to failure and simply give up?

Well, yes and no. There are certainly some things we should give up, such as strategies that don't actually work (more on that later). But it would be wrong to see this as surrender.

What it does indicate is that being successful in any sphere of life clearly comes down to quite a lot more than discipline, not in the least part because we don't actually behave as predictably and rationally as we think we do.

HUMAN IRRATIONALITY

In the 1600s, French mathematician, inventor and philosopher Blaise Pascal famously suggested in his dissertation on 'decision theory' that human behaviour was the result of an individual looking at all of their available options, weighing up the pros and cons and then making the most logical decision possible. Of course, this was in the 1600s and there was very little reality television around to dissuade him from his idealism.

More recently, scholars of the behavioural sciences, such as Daniel Goleman in his 'Emotional Intelligence' series, have suggested that we are far more driven by emotions than simple logic and that by developing our Emotional Quotient (EQ), we may better understand what drives human behaviour and belief systems.

This certainly seems to be the case. Everything we do is to some extent filtered through how our actions will make us feel.

Of course, we still post-rationalise our emotional decisions. There are plenty of men in their fifties driving around in sports cars who can tell you all about aerodynamics, German engineering and their marque's racing heritage ... but all they are really interested in is attracting women half their age. Alarmingly, behavioural studies carried out in Las Vegas indicate that this may often be a successful strategy (good news for the ageing gent in a Porsche or Ferrari then).

Hot on the heels of Goleman's research is the work by Simon Sinek, who tries to narrow down our emotional focus to dealing with a single question — 'Why?' — a question that he rather neatly dovetails into the subsequent questions of 'How?' and 'What?'

This echoes the earlier work of Friedrich Nietzsche and of Viktor Frankl, who, in *Man's Search for Meaning*, asserts that one can achieve any 'what' if the 'why' is large enough.

All make a compelling case for the importance of developing and buying into a clear and inspiring 'Why?' This has certainly been a significant part of our leadership strategy during our combined 50 years in the commercial world and it is abundantly apparent in other people whose leadership we most admire.

However, as anyone who has ever been on a diet can attest, 'why' is often temporary. Initially the 'why' — be it a high-school reunion three months hence, or a wedding, or a hot date — will inspire enormous amounts of action and even results. But, inevitably, time goes by and the 'why' fades. All of a sudden, we find ourselves back on the sofa in our sweatpants, watching *Oprah* and eating chicken out of a bucket!

Why? Good question.

It turns out that, like discipline, an inspiring 'why' can be difficult to maintain over the long haul.

A lot of this is driven by our sense of Identity Congruence, our innate need to behave in a way that aligns with our sense of self. If the 'why' or the program of discipline conflicts with *who* we think we are at our core, it is highly unlikely to be sustainable.

However, it is also a function of the environment and systems we create around ourselves. Discipline is a lot easier to maintain in an environment that supports it. Abstinence is relatively easy when you're an overweight, bombastic senator with nothing on offer (versus being a charismatic President such as Bill Clinton). Eating fresh food is simple in the absence of fast-food options in your local area and workers without families in remote locations are more likely to be willing to put in a little overtime than those surrounded by other priorities. (Why wouldn't they be?)

People working in business-to-business sales often pride themselves on the rationality of both themselves and the customers they serve. In fact, many scoff at anything other than an order-taking approach to engaging their customers: 'They're not interested in soft sell, they want what they want. It's a necessity'. While we hold an almost fetish-like fondness for office equipment, it does seem a bit of an over-claim to call it a necessity.

So what is it that drives these 'rationalists' of the corporate procurement world? When you dig a little deeper and ask them some provocative questions, the process of buying business-to-business products reveals itself to be anything but the straightforward, rational process that its participants claim it is.

Do they buy the best product? No? Then perhaps they are not driven by a rational need for quality.

Do they buy the cheapest product? No? So it seems they're not driven by a rational need for economy either.

The truth is, if they are lazy, they buy what they have always bought; if they are fearful, they buy the best known brand (remember, 'no-one ever got fired for buying IBM'); if they are the typically disengaged middle manager, they don't change things until someone higher up the chain complains. Of course, the list of causes goes on and on, but very few lead to the world of rational decisions that Pascal promised.

These compromised decisions even follow us into our personal lives. A restaurateur once shared with us that if you have an oversupply of a particular wine, you should present it on your menu as the second least expensive option, something they referred to as the 'first-date' wine. The paying partner's 'logic', they claim, runs along these lines: things may not go well, so they don't want to waste money on the really good stuff, but of course, looking cheap may decrease the chances of things going anywhere at all. So they assiduously avoid the cheap plonk and opt for the second most expensive option ('A very good choice if I may say so, Sir').

BELIEFS ARE HARD TO SHIFT

So, if discipline is hard to maintain and our rational minds are little help, perhaps we can enlist the help of belief systems.

Of course, this is easier said than done. Yet this methodology—the shifting of belief systems—has come to dominate in the spheres of leadership, psychology, marketing, sales and performance coaching.

We talk about changing our beliefs in such a casual way that it makes us seem ignorant of just how powerful these beliefs actually are. Many of our beliefs have proved stubbornly hard to move in even the slightest terms over the past few millennia and have in fact led to wars, murder, family breakdowns and even suicides. Nevertheless, it seems to be a logical place to start.

One of the main problems with most campaigns around behavioural change, be they commercial, government or personal, is that we do tend to focus *only* on shifting beliefs. We employ communications campaigns, advertising, keynote speakers, audio programs and the like. However, try as we may to bludgeon our beliefs into submission with affirmations, rational platitudes and emotional blackmail, the beliefs prove to be the cockroaches of the mental world—impervious to even nuclear attack!

Almost every one of us can name at least one thing in our lives that we believe down to our toes is bad for us, self-destructive, unhealthy or emotionally heart wrenching. We know we should stop doing it and yet, despite all our affirmations—sticky notes stuck to the refrigerator, extra coaching sessions and seemingly rigorous strategies to counter this behaviour—we continue to do it.

Part of the reason for this is that our beliefs are very much attached to our conception of ourselves. For example, followers of the various religions do not typically say, 'I believe in the teachings of the Bible' (or the Koran, the Torah, the Bhagavad Gita the Dhammapada)'. They are far more likely to say, 'I'm a Christian' (or a Muslim, a Jew, a Hindu, a Buddhist). For people who are of Jewish ethnicity and Jewish religious belief this is no doubt even more self-defining. What this means is, changing what you believe is not as simple as … well … changing your mind. It actually involves changing your conception of who you think you are.

So what are beliefs in essence? It is helpful to think of beliefs as simply meanings we've attached to the events that occur in life, either through personal experience or adoption through cultural context. Over time, and in accordance with our brain's desire to streamline our very complicated decision-making processes, this distinction tends to get lost and the meanings we've attached to one occurrence start to become more concrete, universal and non-negotiable.

At this point our brains behave very much like The Filter Bubble, which Eli Pariser describes in his excellent book of the same name. We selectively filter the information we seek and then absorb to reinforce these newly entrenched beliefs and simultaneously filter out anything that may challenge them.

This is part of the reason why true diversity is so important in teams. Ethnic, gender and cognitive diversity actually make a group or team collectively smarter. They allow for points of view that would otherwise be missed in a more homogenous group due to contextual blindness.

What this all means is that our beliefs are far more powerful than we give them credit for. But what is more disturbing is that we tend to view our own internal persuasive powers as more than up to the challenge of changing them.

OUR BRAINS ARE OVER-CONFIDENT

Confidence is drummed into those of us who have worked in the corporate world. It is seen as one of the defining characteristics of a leader and its absence is seen as a life sentence of working in middle-meh! So much so, that employees are often rewarded for talking themselves, and their capabilities, up while quietly intelligent souls who come at the world with a dose of wariness and caution are not so quietly sidelined and told, 'Stop being such a downer'.

Of course, there's nothing innately wrong with a healthy sense of confidence or in being engagingly extrovert. In fact, it can be very useful as long as it is supported by a measure of complementary competence.

The reasons why over-confidence evolved in our collective psyche are not completely understood, although perhaps having a bit of swagger and being skilled in the persuasive arts was as important to reproduction in our prehistoric years as it appears to be today.

However, the problems with over-confidence are two-fold. Many of us don't know where confidence ends and over-confidence begins, but more concerning are the small over-confidences we use in our everyday decision-making—the things we don't even process as overly confident. The educated guesses we make, the assumptions we use based on past experience and the little generalisations we cumulatively filter the world through have the capacity to create enormous problems.

Part of this is socialised into us in schools. Whenever a student asks a teacher how to spell a word or what the capital of a particular state is and the teacher replies, 'What do you think?' or 'Try to answer it yourself', they are unconsciously increasing the chances of guesswork becoming a lifelong strategy.

In fact, when we conduct over-confidence tests in the field, asking random passers-by in the street a series of questions they think they should know the answer to—such as, 'How many countries are there in Europe?'—or asking them to point in the direction they think is north, people are far more likely to take a guess than to simply admit, 'I don't know'.

Of course, teachers are not to blame for this; taking chances based on limited information is necessary for human beings to just get through a typical day. This is partly because we don't want to appear ignorant and lose social standing, but also because we create mental shortcuts out of a need for efficiency and rarely have all the information we would like before making a decision. For example, even though we know there is a slim chance a driver may not see the red light as they approach an intersection, most of us still step boldly onto the street when that little green figure appears on the other side of the road without a moment's hesitation. The 'confidence' we exhibit in other people's social conformity, however, can get us into rather a lot of trouble.

Just how much of an issue our over-confidence can be is explored in detail in the book *Confidence: Overcoming Low Self-Esteem, Insecurity, and Self-Doubt*. Tomas Chamorro-Premuzic, a professor of business psychology at University College London, writes that lower confidence is in fact necessary for gaining competence, which obviously sits at the base of genuine confidence. In other words, over-confidence gets in the way of us being curious, asking questions and developing our skills such that *real* confidence is justified.

But the issue is larger than that. When you consider that, statistically, for any endeavour humanity has turned its hand to, half the people involved possessed a less-than-average competency, you begin to understand just what the scale of the over-confidence problem may be.

The dilemma really lies in what over-confidence robs us of. Of course leaders must convey some sense of certainty in order to engage their team to at least attempt to prove a hypothesis right or wrong. It also makes sense that they have a reasonable amount of confidence that their hypothesis is probably correct. However, over-confidence stops us looking too closely at blind spots and possible errors. It has us 'hope for the best' and 'keep calm and carry on' rather than dealing with issues that may completely derail our objectives, regardless of our confidence levels.

LABORATORY CONDITIONS DON'T EXIST

Even when we don't rely on our own prejudices, belief systems and confidence levels and instead do some research into what may be the best course of action, we can still come undone by the environment we choose to test in.

Entire industries exist to help mitigate the mistakes we may make in our endeavours. Researchers, social scientists and strategists of all sorts test hypotheses, conduct double blind experiments and enlist carefully selected polling of 'typical' subjects, producing reams of data … even big data (the corporate world's new security blanket).

And yet, failure is everywhere.

We have often been wary of the true intentions of much research and testing, suggesting (perhaps unfairly) that this work is largely used as 'screw-up insurance' — in other words, research conducted not to inform, but as a defence should things go horribly awry. An employee or consultant can hardly be held responsible for failure if the research suggested success was a more likely outcome.

However, even when the aspirations and the participants involved in the research are noble and rigorous, errors still persist. Part of the reason for this is the choice of environment in which research is conducted and the margins for error agreed upon. So much of the research people do isn't conducted in the real world and the artificiality of the environments we create can't help but skew the results. For example, if you ask someone about their political ideals in a polling questionnaire, they are likely to want to appear more caring, more intelligent and more interested than they may actually be. As a result, a lot of research suffers from much of the same over-confidence in its results as our own best estimates.

To be fair, big data has started to go a long way to improving this process, given its real-world sourcing, although, like all data, big data is only as powerful as its interpretation and application.

Another possible solution lies in a more scientific rather than corporate view of research; that is, research that's designed to generate information, not conclusions. In other words, rather than looking only to prove a hypothesis, we should also use research as a way of identifying the threats to our hypotheses and the conditions under which this proof may come undone.

So instead of focusing on an outcome, we should be focused on generating outcomes.

WE OVER-FOCUS ON RESULTS

Exacerbating the problem are our goal-fixated cultures. Again, this is a hanger-on from the world of personal development.

For years self-help gurus and business consultants have whipped us into a frenzy with goal-setting exercises and experiences that are analogous to facing our fear—such as walking on hot coals or performing a 'trust fall'—all while they drum into us a mantra of a no-excuses results obsession.

Given the fervour with which the corporate world has embraced this kind of thinking, you'd expect organisations around the planet to be ridiculously over-achieving and ticking off milestones and goals like crazy. But that's not what's happening. In fact, the gap between our goals and our achievement of those goals is glaring.

In 2011, researchers at US management consulting firm Bain & Company found that among the organisations they surveyed, a mere 20 per cent achieve their annual goals and expectations. Once again, as we've seen in our personal lives, this is often interpreted as the failure of the individuals involved while our systems and the process of goal setting itself remain unquestioned.

At sales conferences around the world, inspirational speakers with big teeth and a disturbingly psychotic amount of enthusiasm pump up salespeople, telling them to focus on results with pithy maxims such as, 'Don't make excuses, make results'.

The same empty platitudes are often applied in every sphere of life. To experience this phenomenon for yourself, simply hire a personal trainer or a life coach.

One of the favourite anecdotes of the goal-setting fraternity is the 1953 Yale goal study. The story has it that 1953's graduating class at Yale was surveyed to see who had written goals and who had not. It transpired that only 3 per cent of students had written down goals. Years later, when the class was contacted again to check on their progress since leaving college, it was revealed that the 3 per cent with written goals had eclipsed the personal wealth of the other 97 per cent put together.

What makes this story interesting is just how powerful stories are in building corporate cultures and strategy, but mostly what makes it interesting is that it is completely made up. Yale has repeatedly denied any knowledge of this survey in 1953 or in any other graduating year. Yet this story has been repeated so many times by so many different sources that it has fallen into the category of belief.

As a result, goal setting remains the holy grail of corporate and personal strategy, but more than that, it is often the only strategy employed, which is not to say that goal setting isn't useful or that it doesn't lead to success. In fact, we annually set goals for our organisation and staff and use benchmarks of accomplishment to monitor our progress. The issue occurs when it is seen as a single-bullet strategy.

Buddhists refer to this results obsession as 'attachment' and they frame attachment as one of the roots of disharmony. We prefer to see it more as one strategic strand of many that are available. In other words, a clear goal or result is useful, but it may become a limitation as better options and information become available.

A great example of this is the Indian story of how to catch a monkey. It is said that in order to catch a monkey you have to stake a coconut filled with peanuts to the ground. The coconut must have an opening in it just small enough for a monkey to slip its hand into, so that when it reaches inside, grabs the peanuts and forms a fist, its hand becomes too large to come back out again. The monkey becomes so fixated by the goal that its hand becomes stuck and therefore it is trapped. (The story doesn't explain why you'd want to catch a monkey; we'll leave it to you to add your own editorial flavour.)

What's interesting about this story is that it's a metaphor for how modern goal obsession has affected some of the actual results we've achieved. Poor work–life balance, chronic health issues, family breakups, environmental disasters and artificially stimulated truck drivers falling asleep at the wheel are all examples of goals getting in the way of success. In reality, we actually have very little control over results in our lives. The drunk driver who fails to yield as we approach an intersection, the earthquake that claims our home and even the client who fires us because their marriage is on the rocks and they feel a need to assert power in at least one aspect of their lives: all of these examples, despite the self-help industry's protestations to the contrary, lie beyond our control.

However, what we can control—and this is where we should look for control—is our behaviour and our environment.

FAILURE IS AN ERROR IN DESIGN

We tend to personalise failure when we experience it. For all the corporate world's talk of failure being an essential ingredient to success, it is seldom greeted with the enthusiasm of a student learning a valuable lesson. The language is often reminiscent of the breakup speech, 'It's not you … it's me!'

So instead we look to apportion blame, limit damage and, depending on the political environment we're working in, find a scapegoat.

That's very much how we build our cultures inside organisations too.

So, given that so much of what passes for strategy in the worlds of business and personal development is fraught with faux science, ineffective processes that fight against human nature and systems that set us up for failure, what do we do now? We would like to suggest that we need to change environments and systems, not people.

Rather than ignoring or denying our foibles, weaknesses and bad habits, we should instead be designing our systems with them in mind.

If we assume that failure is simply part of the process (and we should), then rather than planning for the best-case scenario (those days when we are filled with willpower, charisma, clarity and courage) we should instead plan in such a way that we can be successful on days when we are just average, middle of the road or plain old run of the mill. In other words, we need to design for being selfish, scared and stupid.

PART II
Think selfish

'At last,' you say, 'someone is telling me something I've longed to hear!' However, thinking selfish is not about 'me, me, me'. Rather, it refers to understanding that we all filter through some understandably selfish prejudices that are key to motivating people and creating engagement.

Tell me WIIFM
If you want me to care, show me how what is important to you aligns with what is important to me.

Offer a reward
We are all, to some extent, motivated by the famous 'carrot and stick' equation. However, rewards are not always what we expect and they don't always elicit precisely the responses we would like.

Make it enjoyable
After years of telling our staff, our children, our communities and just about anyone who will listen, to work harder, behavioural research is starting to understand how we might make play more productive.

CHAPTER 4

Tell me WIIFM

In a two-horse race, always back the one called 'self-interest'.

Paul Keating

While we may not like to admit it, we're (mostly) driven by self-interest.

Before you get offended and claim that you have in fact grown a moustache to raise money for colon cancer research, protested to save an obscure species that was not even cuddly or cute and on more than one occasion allowed someone into traffic, we're not suggesting that people don't do good for anyone other than themselves. What we are suggesting is that we do a lot more good for others when there is something in it for us too.

Yet all our lives we are taught that someone who thinks of themselves or of their personal gain is self-centred, inconsiderate and in fact, not to be trusted. Additionally, we are taught to act as if the needs and desires of others are of far greater importance than anything we may personally aspire to and that we should instead defer our wishes and tendencies in favour of those of the people around us. However, as with many social niceties, this is just a game of pretend. In fact, in this environment, it is only the openly vain and self-serving who should have our trust as only they possess the courage to be truly honest.

Despite this social construct, when we conduct personality tests where loyalties are tested and connections strained, we find time and time again that the needs of 'me' and 'mine' sit not only consistently above the needs of all others, but also by a large margin.

Even those outliers who stray from the norm and put others ahead of themselves tend to reveal, once we dig a bit deeper, that they too are motivated by self-interest in the form of satisfying an internal definition of self as 'self-sacrificing'.

In other words, whenever we try to act unselfishly at a conscious level, we are in fact unconsciously satisfying our own need to earn social status or to generate something similar to good karma or identity congruence or just plain old 'I am a super nice human being and I have done good today'. Selflessness, it turns out, is just another form of selfishness—but with a serving of self-righteousness to help it go down unnoticed.

This fact becomes important when you want to motivate others or you seek to influence, persuade, sell, lead or, in fact, achieve pretty much any form of behavioural change.

The problem is, while we unconsciously act from the point of view of 'What's in it for me (WIIFM)?' we tend to assume that no-one else does. We're so self-centred that we fail to account for the self-centeredness of those around us. For the most part, the results, as you may expect, are predictably frustrating. Anyone who has driven a car in peak hour knows what it feels like when ordinarily good-natured people imagine what it would be like to have machine guns mounted on the front of their car … and wonder if they should trade up to a tank!

Notwithstanding the universal selfishness of our species, it must be said that while we all process the world through a 'What's in it for me?' filter, this kind of thinking should not inform all of our behaviour, nor indeed how we interact with the world around us. This is principally because just as we're wondering 'what's in it for me', so is everyone else. And this is precisely the point. This thinking should inform our judgement and our evaluation of the events that take place in our lives and help us to develop a capacity to ask, 'What's in it for them?'

The more we begin to be mindful of the selfishness of others, the more powerful we become in terms of creating influence, learning persuasion and building engagement. In other words, the more we accept others' selfishness, the more we tend to get what we want, too! (Feel free to read the last sentence with a maniacal tone, Bwa ha ha ha!)

So, if we are predominantly selfish (and we absolutely are) how may that be a good thing not just for our own selfish gain, but in a community and social-contribution sense as well? And, just as importantly, how can selfishness inform our strategies for engagement, sales, leadership, parenthood and even personal development?

SELFISHNESS CAN BE A FORCE FOR GOOD

At the risk of sounding like *Wall Street*'s Gordon Gekko, we'd like to suggest that selfish can be good ... selfish can be right ... selfish works. Please take note of the small caveat we made by adding the word 'can' to the expressions.

There are a couple of reasons why flight attendants—when they stand in the aisle before take-off to present the all-too-familiar safety demonstration—take the time to explain that it is imperative to fit *your* oxygen mask first!

The first reason is, it works. Failing to fit your oxygen mask first will most likely render you unconscious pretty quickly, leaving you unable to play the hero you so often imagine you could be.

The second, more important, reason is that they are attempting to undo the artificial wiring of your cultural socialisation, which has taught us that it just doesn't look good. All around you is a cacophony of sound: jet engines whirring, people screaming, china and cutlery spilling to the floor. The aircraft is hurtling towards the ground and your nearest and dearest turn to you for a sense of reassurance—or even blind hope—only to find you've abandoned the communal environment of the plane for your own personal oxygen supply. Oh dear!

The truth is, we are so indoctrinated to resist our selfish urges, that if they didn't tell you to fit your oxygen mask first, there is every chance you would die—not as a result of the impending impact with terra firma as much as from the sheer terror and embarrassment of worrying about the opinions of others.

BUILD IDENTITY CONGRUENCE

In order to utilise an understanding of what's in it for those around us, we must first understand the filters and metrics people use to establish value. This is the greatest weakness we have seen in virtually every category of business, NGOs and government departments, we have worked with. Almost everyone can wax lyrical about themselves, their agenda and their needs, but stop them long enough to ask about the people they intend to influence or sell to and the conversation dries up pretty sharply (cue chirping crickets). This, as you may imagine, is a critical issue—perhaps *the* critical issue.

In chapter 3, we talked about the human desire to act in accordance with identity. In our research and work we have found pretty conclusively that identity drives all human behaviour; *we don't act based on what we think we should do, we act in accordance with who we think we are.* This is such a critical point that it bears making twice.

If you have an identity that conflicts with those you wish to engage with—whether it be your beliefs, your product, your brand, your intentions or even the people you associate with—it is incredibly difficult to have any real influence beyond coercion.

And so, in order to drive change or engage a particular constituency, it is vitally important that you know both who they are currently and the identity they wish to project to the world.

This is one of the conflicts that businesses that play the price game fall into. Take for example the discount furniture companies that like to advertise with messages saying, 'We're cheap ... really cheap ... so cheap you can't find cheaper!' Of course, while most of us don't mind saving a few dollars, very few of us want our cheapness (which often translates as a lack of success) projected to the world. Such is the fear of being a complete cheapskate that some customers who shop at these stores have been known to ask for their furniture to be delivered in an unmarked van ... under the cloak of darkness ... Clearly not ideal.

If you want to engage and change human behaviour you need to link your goal to their identity and this process starts by aligning your values.

CREATE VALUES ALIGNMENT

As all human behaviour is driven by our identity, so our identity is driven by the values and belief systems we collect or adopt over the course of our lives. Few of us possess the ability to act in a way that is in conflict with our values for any sustained period or with any great success. However, if a cause aligns with our values, we are capable of heroic acts of the extraordinary, discoveries that drive the human race forward, and performance that challenges our very notion of human limits.

But these values can also drive us to commit acts of unparalleled corruption and evil. But, when aligned with our values, these acts do not seem evil at all. They may even be considered of the highest moral value and social contribution. And that is precisely the point: our values drive us internally and consistently and are self-sustaining when linked to a compelling identity.

Dan sits on the board of the anti-violence against women White Ribbon Foundation. This organisation was founded in response to a single heinous act. On the afternoon of 6 December 1989, a man walked into the École Polytechnique in Montreal and massacred 14 of his female classmates. His actions traumatised a nation and brought the issue of violence against women to the forefront of our collective consciousness.

Two years later, a handful of men in Toronto decided they had a responsibility to speak out about and work to stop men's violence against women. As a result, the White Ribbon Campaign in Canada — held between 25 November and 6 December — has become an annual awareness-raising event.

In 1999, the United Nations General Assembly declared 25 November as the International Day for the Elimination of Violence against Women, with a White Ribbon as its iconic symbol.

How Dan came to work as an ambassador for the cause and then sit on its board in Australia is an example of how a capacity to align with someone's values creates change and engagement, and calls on those who can, to lead.

In 2011, Dan was asked to speak at the Sustaining Women in Business (SWB) conference, which was to be held in Adelaide, South Australia. He was flown in to speak on a panel as one of the 'token males' in the room on the subject of 'A woman's place is...'

In the days before the conference, we were discussing what angle Dan should take in this debate (as well as why he had demonstrated such poor judgement in agreeing to participate in a debate with this title in the first place).

Just when the whole thing was beginning to look like a folly, Kieran's daughter—Dan's goddaughter, Darcy—who was two at the time, climbed over Kieran, wrapped her arms around Dan and said, 'I love you, my Dan'. At that moment, Dan had his argument, an argument that had been struggling to form in his mind since he was a 19-year-old student at university.

Two days later, when Dan joined the panel at the SWB conference, he revealed the story of his goddaughter's timely encouragement and told the story of when, as a student, a poster in a textbook had changed the way he saw the world. The poster, which advertised the Violence Against Women Coalition in the United States, had been created by Tom McElligott and Nancy Rice of the 1980s creative hot shop Fallon McElligott & Rice in Minneapolis. It was simply art directed in black and white with bold typography that punched out the headline, 'One in four women will be raped in her lifetime. Will it be your mother, your sister, your daughter or your wife?'

The room watched Dan in shocked silence. Dan went on to say, 'What makes this such an extraordinary piece of communication, one that has haunted me for 20 years, is not that it makes the case for women's safety, but that it makes women's safety a man's issue … it makes women's safety *my* issue'. Such is the power of aligning your values with those of your constituents.

This understanding later informed some work we did to raise money for cancer awareness and research. When we learned that one in three people will contract some form of cancer in their lifetime, we realised that the statistic was so enormous that the other two in three must surely know someone with cancer. This was the strategic underpinning of the work we undertook. We didn't ask people to help strangers; we asked them to honour someone they knew. The campaign quintupled the amount of money raised for cancer research in previous years.

What this demonstrated to us was that a call to act out of self-interest and personal connection was a far more successful strategy than simply expecting people to do the right thing, act out of guilt or simply be generous.

The key is to frame what's important to you in terms of what's important to them. Until you do, you are not in a relationship, whether personal or professional. This is the most critical distinction any leader, salesperson, entrepreneur, partner or parent can make and yet it is a wildly undeveloped skill in most of us. It is perhaps the most common cause of conflict in relationships. It's not that we can't appreciate the importance of someone else's needs; it's that we mostly don't even consider them because we're too busy waiting for our turn to talk.

Instead, in often Oscar-worthy performances, we scream at our children and subordinates whenever they don't do what they're told and we struggle to understand why the world doesn't revolve around our desires. We bury our heads in our hands and sigh with an exasperated, 'Why? Why? Why?' (We probably deserve an award for 'Most unsupporting actor'.)

The truth is, when we align our values with those of others, not only are they more inclined to 'fall into line', they are more likely to pursue our goals with enthusiasm because, essentially, they see these goals as linked to their own.

DEMONSTRATE A CONNECTION TO BROADER GOALS

Before we can anchor our values and desires within the values held by those we want to engage, we also need to understand the goals and desires they hold for the future and the personal metrics they use to measure success.

What this means is we have to link our goals to their personal goals. This is easier said than done as so few of us take the time to truly delve into what motivates those we share our lives with and how well their goals align with our own.

According to Gallup's 'State of the American Workplace' research, released in 2013, approximately 50 per cent of the US workforce is not engaged in the work they do. Twenty per cent is actively disengaged, which means they are probably checking their Facebook updates while you are giving that 'motivational' ra ra speech.

But this disengagement is far from an American sentiment linked to the US economy's recent performance or lack thereof. In fact, this pattern is reflected in workplaces around the world and in many cases, the level of engagement is far worse. The study was conducted in 142 different economies and revealed workplace engagement averages worldwide at about 13 per cent. We hope you weren't planning anything that relies on widespread enthusiasm!

Given the size of this disengagement, you may, quite reasonably, be prompted to ask, 'Why did they apply for the job in the first place?' and perhaps just as importantly, 'How can we reawaken that sense of anticipation now that they've been in the job for a while?'

SHOW THEM WHAT'S IN IT FOR THEIR COMMUNITIES

According to Nielsen's 2012 Global Trust in Advertising report, approximately 90 per cent of us rely on friend recommendations before making any major decision: the suburb to live in, where to send our children to school, whether to take a new job or not, major purchases, even the politicians we'll choose to 'anonymously' vote for. 'Rely' is a powerful word. It means more than just ask for. It means more than simply consider. It indicates that our social set, our intimate network is a critical factor in the decisions we make.

Those of us who seek to have influence—leaders, marketers, salespeople, parents, spouses—can't succeed by speaking only to individuals; we must also engage the connections that sit around these individuals.

In addition to considering their identity and how it is informed by their personal values and goals, we also need to consider the selfishness that drives their social set. Which needs and wants are met by membership in their communities and networks that they cannot have met in any other part of their lives? Do your goals and ambitions align with them or conflict with them? Where is your common ground?

What the Nielsen research indicates is that we form collaborative opinions. This is a key point: people want to collaborate and be involved in processes. And yet, when we want to persuade, influence or engage we typically try to cajole others into accepting our foregone conclusions rather than inviting them into the process while opinions are still forming.

This is not some new-age mollycoddling that is best left to those who live in communes; it is critical to increasing levels of engagement and enthusiasm and, importantly, it creates a sense of ownership. It means our staff tend to work harder, our customers become more loyal and we all begin to internalise the belief system surrounding the work we're engaged in.

We even share our selfishness. Now before you point out that this is an oxymoron, what we're talking about is our tendency to generate collaborative selfishness. In other words, our social networks help to inform what is in our interests and they help us decide whether something aligns with this self-interest or not.

So, if we are to be influential in the lives of others, whether it be our family, our staff or our customers, we have to also influence their social network—we have to influence the influencers!

Group dynamics too are motivated by self-interest. You need look no further than the nearest one-eyed sports fan who believes every umpire is an idiot and needs their eyes tested and that the opposition team is filled with morally bankrupt cheats, the same is true of nationalist politicians who campaign along the lines of 'my country right or wrong'.

What's important to note in this regard is that this shared self-interest enables us to believe we're not selfish at all. After all, if I'm ultimately working for the greater good of the group, even if I stand to benefit, is that really being selfish?

This distinction becomes important when we're seeking to motivate people towards action because, while we may be selfish, we don't like to see ourselves as selfish so we create 'happy delusions' around our behaviour and ultimately frame it as a contribution.

However, anchoring what's important to you in terms of what's important to them (and their social circle) is incredibly important and, for a leader or influencer, it is critical.

OFFSET THE COST

Isaac Newton's third law of thermodynamics states that 'for every action there is an equal and opposite reaction'. For you physics phobics out there, one way of looking at this law in a less physics-like manner is to consider that for everything we create, something is destroyed or redeployed in a way it hasn't been before. For the purposes of this chapter, consider that for every 'What's in it for me?' there is an equal 'What's it going to cost me?' that needs to be considered, and if possible, offset.

It is an almost reflexive response when someone believes they are being sold a product or an idea for them to do some mental arithmetic — a negotiation between cost and benefit. And yet, so often we act as if this is not understood by all the parties involved.

While it may be true that the precise cost and benefit may not be understood, we all to some extent know that cost *is* involved. We know that if something seems too good to be true, it most likely is and as a result our defences become more alert and attuned. We suddenly feel like prey and unconsciously see the other person as a predator. So, not dealing with the cost of gain can actually exaggerate the cost's importance in our minds.

DEMONSTRATE THAT YOUR ISSUE IS MY ISSUE

In 2012, our business, The Impossible Institute™, was invited to work with the United Nations (in Singapore), the Singapore government and some non-government organisations on strategies for tackling the issue of human trafficking in Singapore.

This is a difficult issue to deal with in a first-world country such as Singapore, because the problem is largely hidden behind great wealth and an overwhelmingly polite society. This also contributes to the larger belief that the issue is 'someone else's problem' or that it happens 'somewhere else'.

Unlike a natural disaster, which is incredibly visible and affects an entire community, human trafficking is, by its very nature, a secretive business.

One of the first strategies we suggested to the Singapore government and the gathered UN consortium was that they change the language used around the issue to make it more human, more personal and more urgent. We suggested using the term 'slavery' rather than 'human trafficking' and that the sex industry be referred to as 'organised mass rape'—certainly not the language that our delightfully polite hosts were used to using, but language they could immediately see made a difference to how they thought and felt about the issue.

This strategy, of course, only goes some way to changing people's attitudes about an issue. To go further, we also had to link the issue to their Singaporean national pride. Singapore prides itself on its role in the South-East Asian region, its clean streets, its almost obedient population and its status as a first-world nation. We also suggested framing this criminal activity as damaging the status of the nation and the international image of its citizens. Can a first-world country truly be called first world if it lives off slavery?

This strategy is designed to change the balance of the cost–benefit equation and quite strongly suggest that the international and economic costs of human trafficking far outweigh the costs of ridding the country of it.

The environmental movement

Why do good ideas and movements fail even when there is a benefit to those they are trying to engage?

Let's start by looking at what we'll call the real inconvenient truth in the environmental movement (with apologies to former US Vice President Gore for distorting the meaning he applied to the same phrase): 'the environmentalism fail'.

One of the reasons the environmental movement has, if not failed, at least stalled and suffered from limited influence, is that its principal argument thus far has been to ask people to save the planet because it is the right thing to do.

Even the phrase 'Save the Planet' is problematic because, the planet itself is in no real danger. It pre-dates humanity and will exist long beyond our extinction, not to mention the fact that there are small organisms living in volcanic outflows in a highly acidic environment that would quite benefit from the acidification of our oceans and the sulphur-rich atmosphere that global warming may generate. No doubt they are busy hatching grand plans for what they'll do when *they* rule the world! A more effective argument is to forget the planet's survival and talk about ours—and again, not just our children's or our great grandchildren's, but *ours*! Not some time in the future when we all drive flying cars and ride hoverboards, but now! Another reason why this argument struggles to gain traction is that it is set in the future (incidentally, this is one of the reasons insurance and retirement savings are such a tough sell—because we may or may not need them one day).

Our immediate environmental costs include increasing food prices, economic failures, damage to our houses as the soil structures beneath them dry out, and an increasing incidence of skin cancer. These are all decidedly personal costs related to climate change in the here and now yet most of the time they are not mentioned.

Gender equality

Another important social movement that has enjoyed less success than it ought to have is the campaign for gender equality. Despite the century of advancement made since women's suffrage, we still live in a world where women earn between 70 and 80 per cent of what their male counterparts do, where women are noticeably absent from political life, even in first-world democracies, and where corporate boards are still playing catch-up despite many governments around the world having mandated quotas and minimum representation for years now.

There are a number of reasons for this. One of these is the shortage of women backing the feminist cause for reasons of cultural belief, the availability of education and even the desire to avoid the 'F'-word label. (Feminism has come to be regarded with similar disdain to the other F-word.) But perhaps more importantly is the fact that the gender debate has largely been discussed by only one gender.

In fact, the advancement of women has been positioned as something for women as opposed to being an advancement of the whole of society — something to fight for. Even the notion of having to fight for it suggests a resistance and an opposing side. As a result of this men have not been engaged at all. Instead men have been told that they are wrong, that they are to blame and must be punished, and that gender equality will cost them power or money and position (not to mention angry slurs such as 'misogynist pig'). Perhaps there would be greater success if men were instead made aware that female equality helps make all of our businesses, lives and futures more successful. This would also be a far better strategy for driving change or engaging those who currently hold the institutional power.

THE REAL QUESTION IS, 'WHAT'S IN IT FOR THEM?'

We work with a lot of professional sales teams around the world and what is glaringly obvious, regardless of culture or corporate style, is that salespeople know their products inside out but usually have a thin veneer of understanding when it comes to the people they're trying to engage.

The same is true in personal relationships. We often understand exactly what we're trying to gain but seldom do we have more than a shallow understanding of what the people we're trying to persuade or engage value or are interested in.

This is even more evident in the way we often deal with children. While in public, we often do whatever it takes to keep them happy (or, more accurately, quiet). However, because we are culturally conditioned to think of their wants as insignificant compared with our very grown-up and important needs—including such things as the fact that we're in a rush because we're poor time managers 'so would you please hurry up', or worrying about what complete strangers may think of us to the point where we reprimand children despite their very normal demands ('Too bad, small person. Your bladder is of scant concern to me. I have a social image to protect.')

Thinking Selfish is not about acting selfish; it's about using this understanding of our natures. So perhaps we should end this chapter with a warning: One of the risks of advising people to 'Think Selfish' is that they may read and understand this to mean 'Think Selfishly'. The distinction is rather an important one. Thinking Selfish is to listen, to enquire, to watch, to learn and to honestly appraise what drives most human beings most of the time. In fact, Thinking Selfish is quite the opposite of Thinking Selfishly.

APPLYING 'WIIFM'

When applying 'WIIFM', remember the following:

1 Understand that we are all selfish.

2 Align your intention with the identity and values of those you wish to influence.

3 Frame what is important to you in terms of what is important to them.

4 Link your success to the success of those you wish to influence.

5 Demonstrate how you serve communities and networks as well as the individuals in them.

6 Acknowledge and offset the cost to them (they are aware of the cost even if you are not).

7 Don't act selfish. Learn to accept the selfishness of others and use it. Ask, 'What's in it for them?'

CHAPTER 5

Offer a reward

The day is coming when a single carrot, freshly observed,
will set off a revolution.

Paul Cezanne

The eternal analogy used to describe the science of human engagement and motivation is known simply as 'the carrot and stick approach'. This, however, is underpinned by the somewhat more sophisticated principle of pleasure and pain, which are the twin forces that drive us through a combination of push and pull or, put more coarsely, through coercion and enticement.

ON CARROTS AND STICKS

Certainly, this is a principle we come to understand very early in life. In an effort to control children's behaviour—or at least to minimise our embarrassment in front of those witnessing said behaviour—parents enlist the twin strategies of punishment (which ranges from threats, or sadly at times, the use of physical violence) and reward (which either runs to instant gratification or a promise of gain in the future). These rewards typically manifest as bald-faced bribery, which is ironically a practice that is defined as immoral and even reprehensible behaviour as we grow older. Hence our often strained relationship with the theory.

So while the, 'Do you want an ice cream or a smack?' mentality seems a little outdated (although today, ice cream is passé as parents instead offer their little digital natives some screen time or a new app), this parental manipulation is mirrored in the world we see around us: at school as we learn to navigate our environment and play games with our peers, in our interactions with mainstream media, in the work we do and even in the family unit and the way it acknowledges or punishes us.

Love, or at least attention, is one of the first 'rewards' we *learn to earn* based on delivering certain approved behaviours. Interestingly, we learn to manipulate others by trying to second guess how they may want to manipulate us. Is it any wonder human relationships become so complicated and political? This is not to say that these methods are wrong or that they don't work, merely that they are perhaps becoming less effective in a world where every child either gets an 'encouragement' award or 'naughty corner' discipline.

And yet, despite reward and punishment falling from favour in modern parenting books and new-age management theory, they still very much underpin the reasons we do the things we do and affect us in a particularly visceral way. Our animal instincts still lie very close to the surface, it seems.

Wielding the carrot

Here we will deal more with the carrot than the stick and more with gain than loss as a motivator. Our reasoning for this is two-fold.

First, reward is the facet of this two-prong motivation strategy that we seem to least understand and therefore utilise: we're a lot better at punishment and negative motivation than we are at delivering acknowledgement (our love of the word 'no' pays testament to this).

The second reason is that in a litigious society where 'traditional' parenting and old-school, passive-aggressive management techniques are increasingly frowned upon, punishment is a tool that is becoming more and more limited and, in some cases, quite illegal.

This is not to say that punitive motivation doesn't still have a function in our society. In fact, both must come into play in one form or another. However, as the scope of the negative is increasingly prescribed for us in legislation and social convention, positive reinforcement offers us the greatest opportunity for impact and for personalising the way in which we motivate behavioural change, our teams, our significant others and even our children.

The truth is, we have always been motivated by rewards. Every religion and philosophy offers its own slice of positive motivation in its doctrines. Even the Greek and Roman Stoics, whose philosophy reflected our capacity to endure or embrace the negative, offered their own reward of sorts in the form of inner peace or at least an understanding and acceptance of our lot in life. Many of the Eastern philosophies, such as Buddhism, offer a similar reward, both in this life and in promised lives to come. In fact, religious rewards often seem so extraordinary when compared to the ordinariness and pain of everyday life that they can drive a feverish devotion even though no-one has actually seen or experienced these promised rewards (or at least, no-one has come back and talked about them).

Carrots for conformity

And so, this thinking has informed much of how we organise ourselves as societies and cultures. In order to enforce social cohesion and conformity, deviation from the norm has been punished throughout history, often brutally, whereas the converse — blind obedience and loyalty — has almost always been rewarded through status, remuneration, livestock, shells, rare minerals, religious affirmation, sex and even other human beings (many of these rewards are now considered illegal in more enlightened times).

More mindful, internalised and ultimately more exciting rewards have motivated humanity to perform acts of the extraordinary. Rewards such as notoriety, advancement, freedom and profile have propelled engineers to give us the first powered flight, inspired athletes to break the 'impossible' four-minute-mile barrier, driven civil-rights advocates to challenge outdated beliefs about the value of human beings or long-held prejudices, and encouraged entire nations to change models of government and the distribution of wealth and power.

Perhaps the most iconic demonstration of reward-based motivation throughout history, however, has been the Olympic Games. Traditionally, superior athletes were awarded a laurel to wear on their heads, which conferred status and recognition. In the modern incarnation of the Olympic Games we reward not only the first-place winner of each event with a gold medal, but in the words of comedian Jerry Seinfeld, we also acknowledge the 'first and second losers' with silver and bronze. The obvious humour of Seinfeld's observation aside, it points to the power of rewards to spur us forward to greater heights and achievement.

In school we receive merit awards; in workplaces we receive increasingly long and fancy titles or have our photograph posted for public viewing so that people know we are 'employee of the month'. In our relationships, we engage in various forms of bribery and exchange different forms of value to either generate some attention or, as the relationship ages, to ensure that we get a little more time to ourselves, with no attention.

So why does this reward-based motivation work on us to the degree that it does and what are its limitations?

It's hardly surprising that this has been our model of motivation throughout the millennia as we do, in fact, live in an incredibly competitive world—not just competitive for our increasingly limited resources, but at a very basic survival level for a mate, for love, for a feeling of safety and for solace. Even our most basic needs of food, shelter and sex pretty quickly adopt a carrot-and-stick methodology as we reward the most beautiful, the most physically fit, the most charismatic and certainly the most wealthy when negotiating all three of these essential needs.

Human beings are not alone in this as virtually every species is involved in a competition to earn their version of the carrot and avoid whatever stick is relevant to their rung on the evolutionary ladder.

So while reward and punishment are not the silver bullet of human nature and behavioural motivation (there is no silver bullet), they are in fact critical to our understanding of what sits at the core of our psychology.

THE PSYCHOLOGY OF REWARDS

The works of B.F. Skinner and Viktor Pavlov offer some of the most famous treatises on the psychology of rewards and their research has understandably informed many of our opinions on stimulus/response thinking in the commercial world too.

In short, their animal experiments and human observations — though many seem utterly immoral when seen through modern eyes — have supported and reaffirmed many of the hypotheses of the carrot-and-stick school of motivation.

It is worth remembering, however, that just as their methodologies belong to another age, so too do the contexts of their samples' baselines (in other words, the simplicity of their subjects' needs and the meagreness of their day-to-day lives) contribute to the baseness of motivation required to achieve their results. In other words, punishment and reward work better in poor, undeveloped communities, but as needs give way to wants, the drive to achieve shifts somewhat.

Much of the reasoning of the commercial world still reflects Pascal's 'decision theory' model, that human beings make largely linear and logical decisions. This theory has since been renovated with a fresh coat of psychological paint and by less mechanistic models of human psychology. However, this essentially 'nuts-and-bolts' approach to human engagement has remained stubbornly entrenched in business, due in no small part to the generations of management staff that would love nothing better than for human beings to behave like well-oiled machines.

More recently there has been much psychological research and debate in the realms of performance and motivation driven largely by corporate funding as people continue to stubbornly refuse to act the way academics and clinicians claim they should.

As a result, new theories have emerged. In fact, it is one of the benefits of 'soft' sciences such as psychology that they offer increasing levels and depths of understanding over time rather than answers that are simply right or wrong. This means they require minds capable of coping with abstracts, not absolutes (a benefit that is often thought to be quite annoying, it must be said).

Daniel Goleman's work on emotional intelligence asserts that our 'emotional intelligence' (EQ) is a far more important factor than rationality in both success and personal satisfaction, and infers that rewards must be emotional in nature if they are to attract the kind of lasting results we seek for ourselves and others. Anyone need a hug?

Dan H. Pink, in his book *Drive: The Surprising Truth About What Motivates Us*, suggests that, beyond simple emotion, we should also consider a portfolio of motivators including autonomy, mastery and purpose — drivers that become increasingly important in nations where basic needs, such as food, are in fact in over-supply.

However, it must be said that rewards are still incredibly important in Goleman's and Pink's worlds; it is just that the rewards have, in their eyes, started to move up through Maslow's hierarchy of needs. Of course, in even the wealthiest nations, a small hiccup, such as the banking and loan industry's corruption and the ensuing financial meltdown, is all that is required to turn Maslow's triangle into a flat line.

And yet, even though our thinking on what constitutes a reward has evolved, and even though rewards are often only contextually valuable, they still underpin our essential psychology. We still aim to gain and to avoid loss.

It is said that 'money isn't everything' and this philosophy raises one of the critical problems with asserting the usefulness of selfishness and reward-based motivation. The fact is, although selfish, reward-based thinking is a critical part of our human condition, it still does receive rather bad press. Greed and our constant striving for greater consumption and the worship of 'more' have been blamed as the root evil of almost all of our social ills. And it's not just because of Michael Douglas.

But to limit our thinking about rewards to monetary gain or to the accumulation of things is to miss some of the most powerful rewards we can receive — those of the intangible variety.

THE IMPORTANCE OF ACKNOWLEDGEMENT

One of the simplest and yet most effective rewards we can offer in any sphere of our lives is that of acknowledgement. This may be something as simple as the phrase, 'Good job', or 'Well done', but can also extend to more formal assessment and praise of another person's achievements and contribution.

Giving praise seems such a small, even insignificant, thing to do. It almost seems like counsel your grandmother might have offered you as a child — or something you would cross-stitch on a wall hanging — and yet, this deceptively powerful tool of motivation is so often overlooked that it repeatedly comes up in critiques of management teams in 360-degree reviews. These reviews constantly reveal that managers routinely overestimate their own practice of acknowledgement, rating themselves as good or even excellent, whereas their staff typically rate them anywhere between poor to average at best.

Why do we fail to acknowledge?

Part of the reason for this lies in the cultures we have created in schools, in the workplace and increasingly in our models of what family should look like. Each of these spheres has become increasingly competitive and less cooperative over time.

This has happened to such an extent that we are often asked to perform a cultural audit of an organisation as part of designing a performance and collaboration program. When we perform these audits, we almost universally find individuals and even entire departments have KPIs set up in opposition to each other. These conflicting KPIs mean that in order for one to succeed, another must fail, often catastrophically. One of our principle remits in these organisations is to help them build Co-PIs™, measures that not only encourage collaboration, but link it to their own personal metrics as well.

However, acknowledgement still needs to be meaningful. Giving every member of a team an encouragement award or a generic pat on the back not only fails to create real motivation, it often demotivates the team. After all, if acknowledgement is meaningless, and the lazy person everybody moans about gets acknowledged too, then why aspire to it? Just because a reward is intangible does not mean it should not be valuable nor that it should be so abundant that it ceases to inspire.

Organisations such as Small Improvements, a Berlin-based global performance consultancy, have developed software that provides 360-degree feedback and acknowledgement, not just as part of a standard six-monthly or annual review, but as part of a constant, ongoing cultural development strategy. And already they're seeing extraordinary results.

This software delivers a range of acknowledgement-based rewards, often things as simple as earning badges or social currency (something the Scouting movement and the military have long understood). These rewards are designed to help people remember how far they have come or how much they are growing incrementally. Essentially, their goal is to maintain the enthusiasm that employees bring to work on their first day throughout their careers.

The Sydney-based corporate rewards program RED—which stands for Recognise Every Day—is part of the gifting service RedBalloon. It also offers corporate partners a way of rewarding employees in a more innovative and engaging way. Like Small Improvements, it offers a suite of incentives that are part of a reward process which delivers surprise, consistency and scale.

What this speaks to is an understanding we all share instinctively that acknowledgement feels good, but often ignore it as we become consumed by our own agendas, or by the hyper-competitiveness of our corporate or cultural context.

In fact, one of the most significant acknowledgements you can offer another person is the question, 'What do you think?' This simple phrase can rouse an individual of any age or rank to lift their game exponentially. If there were only one engagement strategy you chose to use in your personal or professional life, it should be this. Not only does this simple question acknowledge the presence of another person, it also recognises their capacity to contribute value. This, it turns out, is critical to making them feel valued, *don't you think?*

REWARDS MUST BE VALUABLE IN CONTEXT

The Western world's default position for rewards is monetary, or at least that rewards have monetary value. In truth, this is a far too narrow view of rewards as many reward systems only have value—and only make sense, for that matter—within a tightly defined context. A child's illustration offered to their parents as a gift of love has obvious worth to the parents even though others may consider it worthless.

However, context extends well beyond parenting and personal connections. Highly contextual rewards can increasingly drive performance too.

Most people are familiar with the martial-arts belt grading system. While in most traditional arts, practitioners remained white belts until they attained the much sought after black belt, modern iterations of these arts now grade practitioners from white, to yellow, to red, to green, to blue and so on, until they achieve mastery and move through further grades to a black belt.

Each colour is associated with an increase in skill level and denotes status within the dojo, or school, but more importantly it is an acknowledgement that promotes interest and dedication.

This incremental grading is still evolving in the martial arts of today. The Brazilian Gracie family, who dominated the Ultimate Fighting Championship (the largest mixed martial arts promotion company in the world) for much of this sport's existence, have been known to add further increments between belts by adding stripes of electrical tape at the end of the belt to indicate progress or to induce greater focus. For instance, when a young martial artist begins to become distracted, something as simple as a stripe of tape helps them return to their practice of the art with greater enthusiasm and attention to detail. Who would have thought sticky plastic tape could be a valuable tool for motivation?

The practice of rewards is reflected in game theory, with the incremental rewards commonly used throughout the video game genre to maintain interest and indicate progress now also being applied to corporate training and development. Again, it is not the reward itself that is significant, it is the fact that the reward is given and the meaning that is associated with it.

THE GREATEST REWARDS ARE UNEXPECTED

Whenever Dan is asked, 'What would you like for your birthday?' his (obviously sarcastic) answer is always the same: 'A little thoughtfulness on your part might be nice'. Apart from reducing the number of people who feel inclined to give him a gift for his birthday, this response does occasionally lead to a more sensible discussion of what makes gifts valuable. In other words, if we have to pick our own gift, or if we know that a gift is coming, does it reduce the sense of anticipation and the perceived value of the gift, and similarly with rewards, reduce their effectiveness as a motivator?

In this regard gifts and rewards work in a very similar way. The expected ones tend to fade from our memories, but we will talk about the surprising examples for years to come. In fact, this is how we editorialise all of our experiences of reality. We manage our memories not in a chronological or even a hierarchical way; instead, we allocate memory to the things that stand out, whether good or bad, even to the point of editing out occurrences that are valuable but not very extraordinary. The truth is, we simply haven't got the bandwidth to consciously remember everything that happens to us, so we mostly judge and select those moments that are 'outliers' (to use Malcolm Gladwell's term) in our experience, principally because they weren't expected or they varied from the norm.

This is partially driven as an evolutionary hangover: we are conditioned to notice changes in the environment and in people around us as a way of protecting ourselves against unexpected threats and in order to identify opportunities for gain. It's why we can spot an available parking space across five lanes of traffic.

The unexpectedness of a reward, whether it be in terms of timing, scale or novelty, increases its value and its potency.

THE DIFFERENCE BETWEEN 'MORE' AND 'BETTER'

The current 'more' or 'better' debate affects more than our sales theories and our management styles. It underscores the current question about which one is a more sustainable metric for success.

This is where the breadth of our definition of rewards is critically important. Rewards are non-linear; in other words, they don't necessarily accumulate or use resources in a consistently increasing way. A reward that is thoughtful, even though it may be resource light, may confer greater value and achieve a greater response than simply upping the ante.

Conventional motivational research, like much of our thinking in our personal lives, has posited that more is better. Even if this is not something we vocalise, it still informs our decision-making. You need only witness the enormous homes of many people in the first world, filled so far beyond what they are capable of holding that the self-storage industry is booming ('I just don't know how we're going to fit three people in a five-bedroom house!').

As we veer towards having everything we could possibly need or want, rewards—or at least more of the same reward—begin to lose their effectiveness. Certainly, we are more inclined to work hard or strategise around gain when the gain relates to something not already in our possession.

This tendency is also seen in the way we raise children and reward them in activities such as sport and academics. One of the constant criticisms we hear about modern parenting is that when you create a situation where no-one can fail, everyone is equally special and rewards are granted for behaviour that is in no way exemplary, then these rewards come to mean nothing and, therefore, no longer provide the motivation they once did.

Unfortunately, this does not suggest that we are sensible enough to appreciate the things we already have. Far from it. It simply means that our desire and motivation decreases as needs shift to wants. In truth, the shift from need to want is one of the most significant shifts within the marketplaces of the first world. It affects how we motivate, how we sell, even which products and services we bring to market. It also changes the value of these products and services from tangible or utilitarian to intangible. In other words, the value of a 'badge' can be greater than a 'gift' with some functional or intrinsic worth.

WHEN REWARDS STOP WORKING

Rewards can only take you so far. Dan Pink observes in his book *Drive* that once a certain level of wealth — or at least comfort — is reached, rewards begin to lose their potency as a motivator.

What's also true is that, occasionally, big and ostentatious rewards can actually be a de-motivator. We often see this in promotional marketing practices. For example, in an attempt to entice you to buy more product, an organisation may be tempted to sweeten the deal with an offer such as, 'Every product purchased comes with a chance to win a trip to Disneyland'. Now, assuming you don't mind noisy children and long queues, this usually stacks up as a pretty amazing prize. The problem is that a reward such as this often seems so big that we immediately begin to think we have no chance of winning it, so we don't bother purchasing the product (which ironically, just shortens the odds).

What marketers have learned is that when, in addition to the big reward (say, a trip to Disneyland), there is also a chance to win a stuffed Mickey Mouse toy every hour, we are much more likely to purchase the product that's being sold. Even though the odds of winning anything are still stacked quite a long way against us (depending on the distribution and product circulation in question), the 'achievable' — or, rather, believable — scale of the rewards on offer increases the likelihood that we will engage.

Rewards can also fail when they come across as overt bribery. We may be selfish, but we don't like admitting to it or letting others see it in an unedited form.

One of the potential pitfalls in acknowledging our 'me first' inclination is that it can have quite a disastrous effect on our social standing. While we may really want all of the cake for ourselves we don't want anyone to witness us eating it.

What this means is that bribery can backfire: if we frame 'what's in it for me' in a less than subtle way, it can have precisely the opposite effect. It's like offering confectionery to someone of slightly more than adequate proportions with the phrase, 'You look like you have a healthy appetite'. As much as they may internally long for the temptation on the plate before them, they have just been placed in a position where social convention dictates that they will highly likely act against their will (only to stop by at a convenience store on the way home and scoff down an entire block of chocolate).

In the end, rewards as a tool for engaging our selfishness are on the whole a very simple and necessary strategy, but how they are delivered and valued requires a strategic approach.

APPLYING 'OFFER A REWARD'

When applying 'Offer a reward', remember the following:

1   Acknowledge proactively, regularly and genuinely.

2   Create rewards that confer status in the context of the desired performance.

3   Deliver unexpected rewards at unexpected times in an unexpected way.

4   Distinguish between more and better and err towards the latter.

5   Don't offer overt bribes or publicly acknowledge self-interest.

6   Avoid rewards that develop a sense of entitlement or become generic.

CHAPTER 6

Make it enjoyable

A spoonful of sugar helps the medicine go down.

Mary Poppins

As you begin reading this chapter, we feel we should offer a word of warning. You are about to be subjected to a rather shameless product plug. You may find this surprising given you are neither watching television nor reading a magazine, although given our past lives in the world of advertising, perhaps you don't. Whatever the case, please bear with us as we attempt to explain our reasons for this.

IT'S NOT JUST GIRLS WHO WANT TO HAVE FUN

Kieran is a proud mum to five-year-old Darcy (not exactly one of the psychotic stage mums we have come to know through reality television shows with titles such as *Tantrums and Tiaras*, but proud nonetheless).

Like most mothers with young children Kieran dreads a task that seems to come around with disappointing frequency: the brushing of teeth. Twice a day the same drama unfolds as Kieran tries to a) get Darcy to brush her teeth, and then if the aforementioned is successful to b) get Darcy to brush them for a sufficient length of time to technically qualify as 'cleaning' her teeth (or at the very least until Kieran feels her parental responsibility has been met).

The problem is that brushing your teeth is *sooooo boring* when you are five and there are so many interesting and new things in life to distract your attention. No matter how frequently the health benefits are recounted before the event takes place, facts fail to impress.

'The tooth fairy likes shiny, clean teeth' is an occasionally helpful white lie but this is mostly in times of wobbly teeth, which have thus far been rather limited.

Enter the musical toothbrush.

This clever little invention is an all-singing, all-dancing number that plays music loudly inside your head. We won't bore you with the science of why things are louder inside your head because all you need to understand is that, rather like when you munch on potato chips, it sounds *fortissimo* (to employ a musical term).

Even more impressive, particularly to a desperate mother, is the fact that the music in question lasts for a length of time that definitively counts as cleaning one's teeth. So Darcy dances along happily as her tooth-brushing experience becomes a mixture of hygiene and happiness—and that's music to Kieran's ears!

What the musical toothbrush provides is what parents stumble across every day in every new negotiation with their children: people prefer to do things that are enjoyable.

Every day, parents, grandparents, teachers and carers all around the world harness the power of fun to get children to do things they would otherwise complain about doing. This includes applying a little creativity to even the most mundane of activities such as making monster faces out of sandwiches. For some inspiration, check out www.funkylunch.com, or if you want to feel completely inadequate, stop by David Laferriere's Flickr page. Astoundingly, this young dad has been drawing 'sandwich art' on his kids' plastic lunch bags every school day since 2008 to get them to eat their whole-wheat sandwiches. It's enough to make mere mortals feel a little inferior in the sandwich department! But wouldn't you be gobbling down carrot and lettuce on wheat too if any of these extraordinary creations were served up in your Star Wars lunchbox?

Beyond simply making the process more fun, parents also use Trojan-horse-like tactics involving covert operations where vegetables are hidden inside any substance with masking capabilities (even Jason Bourne would stand in awe of some of Kieran's 'eat more greens' missions).

As a last resort, should disguises and subterfuge fail, most parents think nothing of losing what self-respect they still possess and shamelessly making strange faces, animal noises or belting out terrible renditions of songs with MC Hammer-esque moves. Kieran often masquerades as a pony named Cinnamon Apples. Cinnamon Apples has been known to cavort down the market aisles whinnying as she pulls the trolley and is fed imaginary apples by her five-year-old Darcy—all in the name of making the grocery shopping more pleasant. Silly, yes. But that's what parents do; whatever it takes to keep our little ones happy, pout-free, tear-free and, importantly, ourselves free from all the drama. Dan, understandably, does not join Kieran on these shopping expeditions.

Parents know firsthand the power of making things enjoyable. No other role in life requires you to be as flexible, creative and entertaining as parenthood. Children, sometimes refreshingly, steadfastly refuse to be 'all grown up' and disguise the fact that they are selfish, scared or stupid. When things are boring, they say so. They also let you know when things are 'yucky', 'not fun', 'confusing' and 'too hard'. When they don't like someone or something, they don't suffer silently or feign interest; they make sure that you and anyone in the immediate vicinity is distinctly aware of their dislike, even if it means lying on the floor of the mall and having a spectacular meltdown!

The upshot of this behaviour is that, rather than always making the behaviour 'wrong', we could look to change the parameters of engagement. What new methods can we enlist to make things so pleasurable that children may actually want to do them? This saves us time, it saves us effort and just as importantly it saves us the enormous embarrassment of being out in public with a whining, complaining and tantrum-prone young one (once again our own selfishness becomes a key motivator).

What we are unconsciously doing, out of necessity, is keeping our audience or 'constituents' firmly in mind and adapting our approach so that we appeal more to them. Instead of wasting energy trying to change every aspect of our children, we alter the task to make the preferred behaviour natural and voluntary.

The question is, can we employ this tactic when it comes to adults, our staff, our customers and ourselves? What if, instead of 'enduring' work, chores and queues simply because we have reached a level of maturity, we found an alternative. Not that we're suggesting we should continue to lie on the floor and scream and kick until we get our way ... although, to be fair, some empirical testing may be warranted.

The good news is that even in the business world, we are starting to learn from the example of our children.

MAKE IT A GAME

The rest of the adult world is waking up to what parents discover out of sheer desperation — that turning the things we 'have to do' into a game is a winning strategy.

'Gamification' — a grandiose title that was originally coined by computer programmer and inventor Nick Pelling in 2002 — is the buzzword permeating everything from education to sales to corporate leadership and management. Simply put, it means to make activities, especially of the mundane or repetitive variety, more appealing and engaging using game theory and practice.

Games can be so much more enjoyable than task lists or should do's. Games still have rules, but just as importantly they also have clear parameters, challenges, victories, rewards and levels. If you fail, you hit restart and try again and again and again. This increases resilience, adaptability and innovation. Games are activities people participate in willingly; we want to level up and gain a sense of achievement and ultimately have a positive experience.

Quest to Learn is a cutting-edge public school in New York City with a curriculum based on game theory. At this school, children learn entirely through gaming — yes, they play computer games all day long (imagine how eager they must be to get homework). Quest to Learn doesn't focus on skills such as handwriting or spelling. Rather, it is obsessed with fuelling kids' desires to learn and discover enthusiastically by embracing the principles of gaming.

The school is not preoccupied with grades and tests but rather with progressing through levels. In a game, instead of pass or fail there is 'try again'. When you apply this model to schoolwork, it becomes far more inspiring. This, unsurprisingly, improves students' confidence, tenacity and engagement levels.

When we worked in the advertising industry, we even 'gamified' the process of idea generation in our agency. Instead of 'working' on a client problem we would play a game. This was especially useful when we were tackling a particularly tricky brief and suffering from blankaphobia (our term for the fear of the blank page that plagues creative people the world over).

The process was simple. We gathered our team around a table and, using the dice from the board game Scattergories, we would roll a letter. For those who have never played Scattergories (you really should) the dice is a 20-sided icosahedron with almost every letter of the alphabet on it.

Once a letter was determined, we then set the game's rather stress-inducing timer (the sound it makes intensifies as time runs out) before generating as many solutions as we could think of beginning with the letter selected. No angst (other than the timer of course). No staring at empty pages. No obsessing over right or wrong. Just fun, a lot of laughter and brains freed from the pressure of outcome and instead only present to the process. In doing so time and time again, we were able to solve tricky problems and break through a cognitive impasse.

Gamification can even help you stay in shape. When it comes to fitness, Nike are the masters of gamifying. With the creation of Nike+, running has taken what was essentially a solo pursuit, and for many of us a begrudging must-do, and made it social and fun. The Nike+

Running app turns your run-of-the-mill run into a good old-fashioned game of tag with other runners who have downloaded the app.

The technology also enables users to invent their own games and hence provide their own motivation. A young man who used to work for us was so keen to get out of the office for his daily run that we had to enquire what fuelled his almost obsessive motivation. As it turned out he was running around the city following a course that roughly mirrored the shape of a penis and testicles. It was something he had been doing everywhere he had lived around the world. He would then share his phallus-shaped route socially proving rather convincingly that gamification is not just for children.

The corporate world is also harnessing the power of making work less like hard work and more like serious play. Organisations as diverse as IBM, Xerox, Samsung, Starbucks, Verizon, Cisco, Target, USA Network and L'Oréal have gamified core tasks.

Pilots, astronauts, anaesthetists, doctors and car manufacturers practise and develop their skills via augmented reality games and inside simulators. Banks even allow investors to practise property investing without spending a single penny. The Commonwealth Bank's 'Investorville' uses real-time data to enable customers to learn to invest without the risk of spending real money.

Even the army is enlisting the power of first-person shooter games to attract new recruits. In his insightful book *Play at Work: How Games Inspire Breakthrough Thinking*, journalist Adam L. Penenberg reveals that the US Army's most successful recruitment strategy has been a video game named *America's Army*. Since its introduction in 2002, Penenberg asserts that the game has amassed more than 7 million players including 40 per cent of new recruits.

It has also helped to shift the public's opinion of the army with 30 per cent of Americans aged from 16 to 24 saying they have a more positive impression of the army simply because of the game. Unsurprisingly, it's not just the US Army that is benefitting from war-game franchises. At the peak of *Call of Duty's* popularity in the UK, young men enrolling in the British Army also reached record numbers.

While 'gamification' resembles the kind of linguistic trickery that would make itself at home in a game of corporate buzzword bingo, this is no passing trend.

Beyond the catchy word, there is a deep truth that we consistently choose the task that gives us greater satisfaction and enjoyment. It is something we have always done. Think of the music that was created by chain gangs to pass the hot, endless and back-breakingly brutal hours.

What this fundamentally reveals is that a strategy that makes no account of enjoyment is no strategy at all.

THE YAWNING CHASM BETWEEN PLEASURE AND PAIN

At the risk of dating ourselves with another 1980s pop-culture reference, we respectfully disagree with pop group Divinyls and suggest that there is not as fine a line between pleasure and pain as many assume. When it comes to making something more appealing (masochists aside), pleasure wins by a mile.

Throughout our history, the pursuit of pleasure has been one of our defining characteristics. One of the earliest known pieces of writing on earth, written not long after the invention of writing itself, talks about the pursuit of life's pleasures: '... fill your belly. Day and night make merry. Let days be full of joy, dance and make music day and night ... These things alone are the concern of men' (from *The Epic of Gilgamesh*).

Even Aristotle, considered to be the father of philosophical thought, mused on our desire for pleasure over pain, and it was a student of Socrates who asserted that pleasure is the highest good. It seems it has always been thus, precisely because human beings are wired this way.

Pleasure, fun, laughter and happiness release a heady concoction of endorphins and dopamine in us. Our own infinite supply of completely legal narcotics then engage our limbic system and have us craving more and more of this feeling. We are all helpless drug addicts jonesing for a fix of feel-good!

Is it any wonder we want our lives to be more enjoyable; our beds softer; our clothes warmer; and our shoes more comfortable, sexy and fashionable than we necessarily need at a hunter-gatherer level?

It is simply a chemical addiction.

THE 'NO PAIN NO GAIN' MYTH

Dear Jane Fonda, although we may have appreciated your lycra-clad, svelte and flexible form, which seemed so unattainable for the majority of us back in the 1980s, you represent a time when attitudes to exercise began to take a decidedly dangerous turn.

The notion of 'no pain no gain', canonised during the era of step aerobics and emblazoned onto countless T-shirts, purports the idea that nothing good comes without working hard and sweating for it.

This idea was not a new one, although when delivered by Ms Fonda it was certainly salient. This philosophy can be traced all the way back to 1650 where in a line from a poem in the work *Hesperides* by Robert Herrick, the poet muses, 'If little labour, little are our gains. Man's fate is according to his pains'.

Yet, despite its obvious tenure in the culture, a myth it is.

A hero's journey does not need to be protracted, tragic, treacherous and filled with tests of character to be successful; this simply adds interest. Our literature and stories therefore tend to reinforce an idealised difficulty and leave us in a mild panic if a thing seems too simple or too enjoyable and suggests that we have somehow cheated or missed something important.

As a result, we shy away from processes that seem too easy or fun and insist on keeping a sense of morbid seriousness in the workplace, because work is work and fun is something…well…different altogether!

Of course, this may not be the most successful way of engaging our staff or customers. Imagine a business plan that suggested customers endure our service (although perhaps you don't need to imagine too hard as many businesses do make a practice of making their customers endure some rather horrific on-hold music, disengaged customer service staff and poor quality products).

When offering a product or service we should instead seek to minimise pain and maximise the feeling of gain. By inverting the statement to 'less pain, more gain' we focus instead on how we may reduce the pain points for our staff and customers.

EAT THE CHOCOLATE FROG

The great majority of us naturally resist hard or unpleasant work. We put it off. We avoid it. It's a universal experience. In fact, Australians have coined a term for this kind of person: they call them a 'gunna'. A person who is a 'gunna' (not to be confused with a goner, which has rather more serious implications) is simply a person who is eternally 'going to' (gunna) do something, but never quite gets around to it.

One of the best-known motivational speakers of the ultra-positive genre is Brian Tracy. His mantra for avoiding procrastination and overcoming inertia is famously, 'Eat that frog!'

What he's metaphorically suggesting is, 'toughen up, precious, and get the most difficult part of the task over with promptly and quickly'. This enables you to start the day with a sense of accomplishment as well as making the rest of the day seem a doddle.

In truth, this is one of the theories within the self-help movement that actually suggests you deal with realities, not ideals, and is therefore quite useful. But perhaps, even in this strategy, there is room for improvement. The problem with eating a frog is that at no point does the frog become substantially easier to eat (our Gallic cousins may have found a way to make this amphibian a gourmet item, but outside France, a frog is a frog).

Eating that frog is rather like willpower. You may be able to force yourself to gulp down its slippery sliminess, but there is always another frog lurking, waiting to be eaten. In other words, as a strategy it is temporary and finite.

What if, rather than simply eating the frog, we asked a different question such as, 'How could this frog be made more appetising?' or, 'What if we made the frog out of chocolate?' In other words, how could we change or reframe the dreaded activity in such a way that it doesn't require the eating of anything we find unpalatable?

The Fun Theory, an initiative sponsored by Volkswagen, has invested rather a lot of time and effort in seeking how to manufacture these 'chocolate frogs'. Their remit is to influence behaviour positively by making the solution to a societal issue fun!

Some of their experiments include fitting a staircase with enormous piano keys that make taking the stairs an enjoyable distraction. They also created a way of making putting rubbish in the bin (and not on the ground) not only a good thing to do but a fun one too. They built a rubbish bin that people would walk out of their way to deposit rubbish into. Every time you drop a piece of rubbish into the bin, the sound effect of a plummeting whistle creates the impression that you have just dropped your rubbish into the world's deepest bin. Not only do people dispose of their rubbish in the right way, they even pick up nearby litter.

We use this thinking as an exercise in some of the workshops that we run with corporations. We divide a page into two columns. On one side we write, WHAT'S THE FROG (every job has one). On the other we write CHOCOLATE FROG. We list the frogs in the business and then set about finding ways of making them chocolate frogs … or, at the very least, carob frogs.

The goal is to turn productivity roadblocks and procrastination points into opportunities for enjoyment. It's a simple and powerful exercise.

FOCUS ON THE BORING BITS

One of the traps we fall into in an effort to improve our performance is our tendency to spend a disproportionate amount of time on the things we're good at.

What we miss in doing this, however, is the opportunity to lift our weaknesses and actually make the boring bits more interesting and perhaps turn them into assets.

Consider what is the most mundane, time-consuming or tedious activity in the work you do. We find this is frequently the moment where you risk losing most customer engagement.

For instance, when you are on the phone to a call centre, it may be the moment where you sit on hold listening to the world's worst muzak compilation, getting angrier and angrier as the already irritating soundtrack is constantly interrupted by a disingenuous voice saying something very much like, 'Thank you for waiting. Your call is important to us and will be answered by the first available operator'. Perhaps, like us, you find yourself thinking, 'If our call is so important, wouldn't it be a good idea to hire enough staff to answer it within a reasonable period of time?'

There must be dozens of ways to make this universal experience less boring and more interesting, or even entertaining. Customers on hold could be given the opportunity to choose the genre of music they listen to or hear new-release music, enter a competition or be directed to a moderated help chat room. Alternatively, some comedy or an inspirational speech could be played.

This is hardly a definitive list, and of course these options all require some work up front, but if this is the point where you lose new customer enquiries, wouldn't that work be worthwhile?

Consider also amusement parks. The highlight of the park is undoubtedly the rides; the worst part, the queues. You may wait for an hour or more for just 40 seconds of joy. So why don't amusement parks have a deliberate focus on the queue experience? Why not develop technologies and experiences that are fun and exciting to engage people so the time passes quickly?

Once you have determined what your 'boring bits' are, it's time to put your energy into making them better. If you can turn the boring or mundane into something extraordinary, you can literally transform your behaviour, your business and your entire community.

Air New Zealand is known the world over for taking what is arguably the most boring part of the flight, the safety demonstration, and turning it into something people eagerly (even repeatedly) watch.

These unconventional safety videos have included staff wearing nothing but body paint, Richard Simmons giving passengers a pre-flight work out, hobbits from Middle-earth stowing their 'precious' luggage and bikini-clad supermodels (the last one attracting more than a little furore).

What is astounding about these safety videos is that they have stopped being something you sleep through or otherwise ignore, and have become something people want to share on Air New Zealand's behalf. The videos now receive millions of views on YouTube and command more engaged inflight eyeballs than any other safety demonstration on the planet. And this is something airlines are obliged to do for insurance compliance!

In the UK, the British Heart Foundation took a notoriously confusing lesson—hands-only CPR—and turned it not only into an enjoyable lesson but also, significantly, into one that is almost impossible to forget.

They did so using English soccer star turned Hollywood hard man, Vinnie Jones. Vinnie addresses the audience and gives us the impression he has seen more than a few folk in need of some resuscitation (if ya know what I mean!) Then he teaches viewers the finer points of CPR: 'Call for help and push down hard and fast on the big gold sovereign (the medallion sitting on the poor chap's chest) to the beat of the disco classic "Stayin' Alive"'.

Not only is it fun to watch, it is incredibly memorable. This instructional film was such a success that the British Heart Foundation commissioned a 'Mini Vinnie' film especially for school kids. If you are going to suffer cardiac arrest, it seems London is the best city for it to happen.

Staying with the Brits, Sir Richard Branson is the master of the 'transform the boring bits' strategy. He applies it to virtually every sector he operates in. Think about the categories in which he has launched businesses. He seems to have built his entire reputation on selecting the staid and boring businesses with awful customer experiences and transforming them into something 'amazing', a word you don't often associate with air travel, banking, phones and health care. What Sir Richard realises is that business does not mean boring.

WHY SO SERIOUS?

So many organisations require their people to check their humanity and individuality at the door. It has been decades since the production-line model of business dominated the commercial world, and yet today we still produce highly average, homogenous employees the way we used to produce products.

Sadly, the world of business seems to mostly take itself rather too seriously. While it is quite true there is often a substantial amount of money involved and people's lives can sometimes be at stake, all business is still the business of relationships, and if we're not careful, those relationships will become incredibly stale.

In truth, serious is no more important than fun. Fun, as it happens, matters rather a lot. Fun has been rather defamed by the worlds of business and government and is seen as childish, insignificant, flippant and a folly. But as we've already demonstrated, play is a vital part of the learning process. Animals naturally play and so do human beings. Our mental state exerts an incredible influence on our health and wellbeing and the importance of fun in this equation is increasingly a subject of research into longevity and performance.

Fun can do things that serious simply cannot. Dan has spent much of his adult life travelling the world, facing rooms full of people, armed with nothing more than his insight and wit as a stand-up comedian. What he has discovered is that humour opens people's minds; they're less defensive and more likely to entertain a new idea—it's what Dan calls 'ah, ha, ha' moments.

Humour enables us to have conversations that would otherwise be uncomfortable. That is the power of comedy—lines can be crossed and boundaries stretched without great consequences. Things can be brought up that would earn a rebuke or even aggression if stated in earnest.

Today, attracting and holding customers and staff is more difficult than ever. It's no longer enough to simply be good at what we do or professional in how we deliver. We must create value beyond the utilitarian and functional. Intangible value is non physical—more emotional—and, like it or not, today we are all in the entertainment industry. People, organisations and brands must do more than simply produce because it is those that can also engage that will win.

Google's 'Googliness' and its willingness to play even with sacred cows such as their logo make it a very attractive workplace option for college graduates looking for an alternative to the Wall Street 'burn out' factories.

Seriousness does not make you any more substantial; it does not give you a safer pair of hands or indeed make you any more professional or important than taking things a bit more lightly. Seriousness has its place, but the 24/7 seriousness we see in corporate life today is a vestige of industries of the past and the employees and customers of the future are, frankly, demanding better.

APPLYING 'MAKE IT ENJOYABLE'

When applying 'Make it enjoyable', remember the following:

1 Harness the power of making any activity enjoyable.

2 Consider your audience and rather than forcing changes on them, change your parameters of engagement.

3 Turn the mundane into a game.

4 Seek to minimise pain and maximise gain.

5 Identify your 'frogs' and consider how you could make them chocolate frogs.

6 Focus on the boring bits and consider how these could become assets, not breakage points.

7 Lighten up and change hard work into serious play.

PART III
Think scared

Fear can fight against inertia, resistance and imagined safety if we learn how to use its power for good. So let's pull ourselves together and boldly step into the unknown.

Flip the fear
Fear is an incredibly motivating emotion. The key is to align fears with undesired behaviour and remove them from the actions we wish to encourage.

Link it to the known
Change is innately scary and for good reason. Throughout our history change has not always been friendly to the human race. So how do we change our fear of change? By linking change to things that are comfortable and familiar.

Show them they're not alone
Human beings are incredibly social animals. We find strength (and comfort and courage) in numbers. Feeling like we are part of a movement around change emboldens us and makes us feel more confident.

CHAPTER 7

Flip the fear

The only thing we have to fear is fear itself ... and spiders![*]
Franklin D. Roosevelt (*Annotated by Robot Chicken)

Is there anything the human species will try to avoid more than fear? Rituals, industries, belief systems and even entire cultures have arisen as a defence against our fears and doubts (not to mention cuddly toys and cute little night lights to keep the dark at bay). In turn, we assiduously avoid situations, people and even times of day that make our skin perspire, our hands tremble and our stomachs churn.

What's more, these fears are often notoriously illogical and even highly unlikely. Comedian Jerry Seinfeld once observed that at a funeral 'most people would rather be in the casket than delivering the eulogy'. Such is our fear of public speaking.

And yet our fears are always with us. As often as we may try to bury or ignore them, they are always lurking around the corner, in the closet or under the bed.

Fears do not always spring from the irrational. Fears of the unknown, of dark alleyways or even of foreigners tend to have some of their roots in historic precedents. An 'unknown' mushroom, for instance, may lead to death by poisoning. Dark alleyways can conceal any number of dangers, including uneven surfaces that may trip us up or perhaps a person with a wicked intent. And, throughout the course of history, foreigners haven't always visited for the purpose of tourism, trade or friendly immigration.

However, in our fear of fear we do tend to amplify the things we are afraid of while simultaneously trying to steal from them their power over us. The truth is, a healthy acceptance of their usefulness mixed with a dose of realistic expectation and wariness, is a far more sensible strategy—and even a productive one.

Fear, despite all its negative connotations, is in fact one of the most motivating emotions a person can experience. We typically think of motivation as being a trancelike state of delirium that enables those who possess it to jump out of aeroplanes or cleave an unsuspecting wooden board in two with a single blow. But often, the emotions we consider to be negative, and thus less worthy, can indeed be incredibly motivating.

This includes emotions such as revenge and avoidance. Even the most basic of fears—those with social repercussions, such as the fear of failure—can be flipped and become a useful motivator when used aright.

So let's turn the lights off, put down our security blanket and delve into an exploration of the unknown to learn how to turn fear into an asset.

FEAR DRIVES CHANGE

The fable of the middle-aged smoker who eats a high-fat diet, includes virtually no exercise in their daily routine, works in a job that requires them to be sedentary in front of a glowing computer screen—all the while ignoring their doctor's constant warnings to change their ways—only to completely change their lifestyle after a life-threatening heart attack has almost become a cliché (as well as a rather grammatically challenging sentence).

However, as easy as it is to judge such a person as foolish (or incredibly lucky for having survived), the fact that this kind of behaviour is universal to the human experience raises an interesting question: Is this in fact the way all of us are hard wired to react? In other words, do we only change when fear flips from 'change' to 'failure to change'? If so, it may suggest that fear could also be our greatest ally when it comes to driving change or increasing our sphere of influence.

Those of us who hit the gym regularly and count fibre and protein portions during the day are often inclined to point the finger at our middle-aged friend as if to accuse them of lacking discipline or even a sense of personal responsibility. The more uncharitable people in this group often bemoan the extra cost and strain the unfit add to our overloaded health system.

Of course, those who are healthy in the physical spheres of their lives are just as likely to neglect the health of their intimate relationships, their businesses, their savings for the future, their children's education, the moral decay of their communities and so the list goes on. That is, of course, until the fear of not changing outweighs the fear of change.

So it seems, while the type of fear may vary, our behaviour around fear does not. People clearly quite enjoy the status quo until the idea of not changing changes everything.

Having observed all of this, it is worth noting that fear also paralyses us like no other emotion. We come into this world with a handful of very primal fears such as falling, being hungry and being abandoned. We then add to this repertoire as we go through life, until many of us have a bucket list of things *not* to do (or that we think we can't possibly do because we are too afraid).

This realisation in turn causes us to berate ourselves and develop a hate and mistrust of fear, which only causes our fears to expand and exert more influence over our decisions and hence our lives.

But what if we were to flip this thinking? What if we began to see fear as an asset? After all, the fear response evolved out of necessity: to keep us safe, to make us wary of changes in our environment, and to persuade us to move on when the landscape we lived in provided fewer options for food, water and shelter. This is fear's legacy to us.

It kept our ancestors alive long enough to breed and it continues to keep those of us sensible enough to heed its credible warnings living, breathing and procreating.

So how do we learn to see fear in a new way, not just in terms of our survival but also as a way of achieving and thriving?

SOME FEARS COST US

Clearly not all fear is good, nor does all fear ultimately end up working as a force for good. Certainly the *Scary Movie* franchise bears witness to that.

Some fears stifle creativity, make us play a much smaller game than we are capable of and keep us from speaking up, smiling at a stranger, rallying our staff to our cause and at times even venturing out of the house. In cases such as these, fear is a far-from-useful emotion and in fact it robs us of what joy we may otherwise experience.

Some extreme levels of fear, and those that develop into phobias, don't simply limit our emotional and intellectual lives, they can also have a devastating effect on our physical lives. The distress an uncontrollable fear can exert on the body can damage our health and age us prematurely. British comedian Ben Elton, who rose to prominence in the 1980s, once admitted to suffering an acute fear of being heckled while on stage and quipped that his body was ageing at different speeds. 'I'm 35,' he observed, 'but my arsehole can remember the war!'

However, as damaging as extreme fears can be, it is our tendency to empower the other fairly garden-variety fears that costs so many of us. And these are exactly the kinds of fears we need to learn to turn to our advantage.

One of the most efficient ways of analysing the usefulness of a fear is to ask the question, 'Is it completely rational?' The rationality or otherwise of a fear is what determines its capacity to be 'flipped'. Although we live in what we may consider to be perilous times, in truth, with medical advances and improvements to our diet and workplace safety laws, we are living in an age that would make previous generations think us soft. Many older people who are still with us today would no doubt agree with that.

So, if we accept that some fears are good and other fears can be destructive, how do we learn to navigate and harness this suite of emotions that we spend most of our lives avoiding? How can we swim with the current, or redirect its energies so we're headed roughly in the direction we would like to be?

To achieve this, we must first understand our fears and learn how they help or hinder us.

The fear of change

The fear of change is an almost universal experience that takes no notice of national or cultural boundaries. And it can manifest quite violently against what may otherwise be seen as reasonably insignificant discomforts.

This, as you may suspect, harks back to the earliest days of humanity. The truth is, sudden changes—be they environmental, human, or even physical—have the potential to be harbingers of doom.

Where this becomes tricky is in deciding whether a change *is* one of 'doom' or something that may in fact improve our lot in time.

The nature of fear is that it doesn't give us a lot of time to sit around hypothesising. In fact, fears are often useful precisely because of their almost reflex nature. As intelligent as we are, human beings tend to overanalyse. Perhaps this is the reason why there aren't more smart people around today (just a theory)!

The fear of change is an issue leaders of all kinds deal with constantly— whether it be a new competitor to the marketplace, new intelligence about an imminent threat, implementing a new software system or even something as mundane as breaking out of an old routine or trying to kick a no-longer-useful habit. Added to this, however, is a more modern experience, that of change-fatigue, a relatively new response that has accompanied our logarithmic rate of change in recent times. What this means is that change no longer simply threatens, it ticks us off too.

The fear of making mistakes

The fear of making mistakes is also a fear of change. The difference is that it is a fear of negative changes that you generate yourself. This fear of making mistakes, which can also manifest as a fear of failure, is the fear we most regret in hindsight.

For their book *What I Wish I Knew at Eighteen*, Dan and his co-author Marty Wilson interviewed hundreds of people to learn what advice they would like to go back in time and give to their 18-year-old selves. The overwhelming majority said they would take more risks, wouldn't play so small and would be less afraid. It was their fear of making mistakes that most of them regretted.

The fear of making mistakes is, ironically, a defence against regret and yet this is also the inevitable result it generates. It's worth noting that ignoring this fear can often lead to regret and even heavy criticism on social media, so it should not be ignored entirely.

This fear reveals itself in our behaviour before, during and after selling and purchasing things too. Fear drives some people so much that just the thought of visiting a car dealer's showroom is enough to make them break out in a cold sweat as they imagine being conned by an overly scented wheeler dealer in a sharp suit. And although they may be happy after the purchase, the sweating reappears as does post-purchase dissonance—that nagging feeling of doubt that we hold in the pit of our stomach when we have time to allow doubts to fester.

In any case, this is a powerful fear that drives other negative behaviours such as avoidance, procrastination and inaction.

The fear of difference

The fear of difference is one of the easiest fears to understand because its origins are so closely related to our natural survival instincts, but it is perhaps the fear that has done us the most damage throughout history—from racism to sexism to the hate crimes that have plagued same-sex relationship equality and even religious wars.

Although it is often underpinned by sound logic, the fear of something different fundamentally robs us of diversity. And diversity as it turns out is critical to a team's performance, resilience, agility, innovation and even intelligence. A study conducted by the Massachusetts Institute of Technology (MIT) into the collective intelligence of groups revealed that the diversity of a group lifts the collective IQ.

As part of that study, MIT took a homogenous group of men and tested their IQ. They then added one woman to the group and tested the group again. The collective IQ of the group went up (we can almost hear the smug sighs of 'of course it did' from our readers of the female persuasion). What was more startling was that as they added more women, the collective IQ continued to rise (big surprise, right ladies?) In fact, the collective IQ continued to increase until the diversity balance flipped back the other way and as diversity began to diminish, so did the collective IQ.

It transpires that it wasn't women making the group more intelligent, it was diversity, because diversity offers us additional points of view. It helps prevent situational blindness—an inability to see precisely because you have too much knowledge of a particular subject, so much so that you can no longer see alternative ways of solving problems you deal with every day.

This makes strategies for dealing with the fear of difference a cultural and community imperative. With no plan in place for reframing the fear of difference, we may not only perform beneath our best and miss opportunities for innovation and original thinking, but critically, we may be blissfully unaware of a blind spot that could end up costing us everything.

The fear of being out of control

Perhaps less obvious, although no less destructive, is the fear of being out of control. This fear keeps us small, contained and operating in a comfort zone that may be considerably smaller than we deserve.

What adds to the irrationality of this fear is that, despite what self-help books like to tell us about personal responsibility and owning the outcome, the truth is, there really is very little in life we do in fact have absolute control over. Although this statement may be enough to start some of you hyperventilating and rocking in your chairs, an alternative response may be to realise that given this information, worrying about being out of control doesn't give us any greater power over the situation.

If we are part of a web of influence, only a fraction of which we control, then it seems logical to control the things that we can and then be prepared for and responsive to those things we do not control. Of course, that is quite an assertion, given how debilitating this fear can be for some people, but questioning the rationality of a fear is an excellent strategy for beginning to rob it of its power.

Having said all of this, as you may suspect, our perspective on fear is that it is primarily a good thing — a force of nature, if you like — and that rather than willing it away or fighting against it in what will ultimately be a futile battle, we should in fact embrace it and use it to our advantage.

LEARN TO SEE FEAR AS A LEVER FOR POSITIVE CHANGE

So if we accept that fear has a lot of downsides, how can we turn this around and use fear as an asset in achieving positive change in order to generate the behavioural change we so desire? How can we generate an opposite fear, one that is linked to not changing?

As mentioned in chapter 2, TEDster Kelly McGonigal and other health psychologists assert that contrary to popular belief, not all stress (which is essentially a fear of possible outcomes) is necessarily bad. They further state that stressful experiences can be used to promote adaptive responses and that individuals can be trained to think of stress arousal as a way of maximising performance.

The long and short of it is, reframing fear as an asset may not only remove impediments to performance, but can actually serve to heighten and lift it.

Fear (and its close cousin, stress) are suffering from some bad PR and really need some rebranding. We all need reminding that sometimes fear has been the good guy, and it has certainly been a considerable asset in the armoury of social change. AIDS awareness campaigns have featured Grim Reapers bowling victims down like tenpins in an effort to shift the fear of not having sex, to having sex, and immunisation and anti-immunisation campaigners have traded blows in a war of fears, each trying to tip the argument in their own favour.

Rory Sutherland, vice-chairman of Ogilvy Group UK, famously tells the story of Atatürk, a military leader in the then Ottoman Empire and later the first president of Turkey, who in an effort to stabilise the food supply added an additional carbohydrate to the mix — in this case potatoes — flipping the fear of eating potatoes into a fear of not eating them. In fact, by decreeing them a 'royal' vegetable that no commoner was to eat, he also ensured that not only was the fear flipped but that a desire to eat them was achieved.

Rather than seeing fear as one sided, these examples show that by seeking to defeat or decrease the fear that was limiting them, people found that a better, or more compelling, strategy was to increase the fear on the other side of the equation.

DEFINE AND CONTAIN FEAR

One of the most useful strategies for dealing with fear is to define it clearly and contain it.

Before we can use fear as fuel for performance we must first understand how we are reacting to it and what its scope of influence is.

Initially, we need to have a good understanding of whether the fear is realistic or not. There's no point flipping a fear if it's 99 per cent accurate and saving us from disaster (physical, financial or otherwise). But beyond whether the outcome we fear is realistic or not, we need to understand whether the thing we fear really is the thing we fear (stay with us, this is not as esoteric as it sounds).

Often when we consult with leaders and organisations, we're surprised to find, once we dig beneath the surface of the problem or issue we've been brought in on, that the perceived problem is not actually the issue at all. Here's an example.

While helping the leadership team of an international bank build strategies for aligning personal and corporate goals, we did some mentoring with George (not his real name as we'd like to respect his privacy).

George indicated that his key personal goal was to be available to pick up his son on the after-school run. We played a game with George that we like to call, 'Act like a four year old', where after every reason George offered in support of the goal, we would say, 'Why?' (as a four year old would, hence the name). After five minutes of this childish questioning, George said, 'Stop! I don't want to pick him up from school. To be honest, I can't imagine anything worse. I just want to be able to spend some time with him talking about what I think matters in life'. And so it is with all of us: the issue we see is not always the real issue we face.

In the same way, the fear we see is not always the real fear. A fear of change may actually be a fear of losing a cherished relationship, or even something as mundane as missing out on a good parking spot or leaving a barista who makes our mornings bearable. The point is, defining the fear, containing it, and defining its parameters and influence are all critical to turning it into an asset.

INSTIL APPROPRIATE FEAR

Clearly, some fears are real. If you find out, for example, that threatening calls you've been receiving are coming from inside your house, there is only so far a reframing exercise is going to get you. Likewise, chest pains, missing children and close calls on the road are not something to be used as practice for mastering fear. Some fears must be dealt with on their own merits.

That said, how can we use negative motivation? How can we put fear to work for us? And where do we start?

This really comes down to how we instil fear that is appropriate both in terms of the nature of the fear and its severity. There's no point scaring yourself just for the sake of it (unless you happen to be into that kind of thing for the thrill of it).

Often this may include actions as simple as listing the negative possibilities of not taking action. For example, the decision to start a new business could be driven by motivating fears such as the idea of having a boss for the rest of your life, never being financially independent, someone else putting your idea into the marketplace before you or losing face in front of your entrepreneurial friends. Depending on your personality type, one of these may just be the leverage you need to prompt action.

As well as running a business and authoring books, we also spend a good deal of our time travelling around the world speaking to corporate organisations, government departments, activists trying to drive social and economic change and entrepreneurs looking to get a business edge.

Kieran, as one of the few female leaders in the world of Mad Men, is in hot demand for ideas on working with human nature and developing intuitive systems. Dan has a 'let's not kid ourselves' style that positions him as a truth-teller on whom executives, directors and boards rely for his candour and insight.

But it hasn't always been this way. In our early years together in business, Dan was an awful presenter. Although he will deny it, he would sit in meetings quietly judging everyone. However, he also knew that a key part of his role as a leader would be addressing his team and the leaders of the organisations he worked with. So he did the only thing someone who is an uncomfortable presenter may logically do: he spent three years touring around the United States, the UK, Australia, Asia and Europe as a stand-up comedian.

Although this doesn't sound particularly logical, his rationale was that if he could handle a hostile, stand-up comedy audience, then a more sedate corporate crowd would be relatively easy to handle, particularly with a subject he was expert in. In other words, by embracing a fear greater than the fear that was preventing success, both fears diminished exponentially.

Having said all this, the primary reason we need to administer fear in appropriate doses is so we can protect ourselves from fear-based paralysis. The principal problem with fear is that it can lead to inaction. In other words, we become so infatuated with the fear that it paralyses us.

We often see this behaviour when charities and public-service announcements try to raise money or awareness for issues that are, by their very nature, intrinsically scary—for example, kidnap, rape, deadly diseases, war and the like. These causes can be so intensely frightening that they make us to shut down and not engage with the message at all.

These kinds of movements often use 'scare tactics' in their communications as a way of eliciting empathy and buy-in and to increase their leverage to 'make the sale'. However, often these tactics are so visceral and frightening that people simply switch off. If we are left with a sense that an issue is too large for any individual to have an impact and we feel like 'there's nothing we can do', that's precisely what we do ... nothing.

One of the ways this fear paralysis manifests is in our tendency to catastrophise the possible outcomes, a behaviour that features quite prominently when psychologists are helping patients deal with stress and depression. In other words, we look for what the very worst outcome of something happening would be, regardless of how long the odds may be of it ultimately eventuating.

This very human tendency was brilliantly illustrated in an advertising campaign for Dr Pepper. One famous example cast Jesse Eisenberg (of *The Social Network* fame) as a young man wandering around a convenience store. He sees bottles of Dr Pepper in a glass refrigerator and thinks to himself, 'What's the worst that could happen?', a question he's about to find the answer to. As he opens the door to retrieve a can of soda the refrigerator's entire contents spill out and pin him down in the aisle. The emergency services are called, and in order to free him, they have to cut off his trousers (you can only imagine the young man's embarrassment). He is then carried from the store by the emergency crew, sans trousers or underwear, and held aloft as he passes giggling teenage girls, a gathering crowd and a camera line while a news helicopter broadcasts his story to the world with the caption, 'Butt Naked Boy'.

This commercial is one of a series of Dr Pepper advertisements designed to point out how ridiculous it is to worry about trying something new, such as a Dr Pepper soda. After all, it's not a massive risk. It's a can of soda! If you don't like it you don't have to drink it and who knows you may find you love it! What it reveals is our deep-seated tendency to expect the worst, even to the point that we fabricate the possibilities.

REBALANCE THE FEAR

This is perhaps the most important facet of this chapter. We are not advocating that you ignore your fears or throw yourself at them as part of a midlife extreme-sport crisis, nor are we suggesting that they are all irrational and imaginary. What we are suggesting is that they can be useful for driving change and shifting behaviour and that this relies on shifting the balance of the fear equation from one side to the other.

For instance, if you were afraid to go for a jog because you're looking a little wobbly around the middle (after a few too many ice creams) and are scared that people might laugh at 'the fat guy in tight-fitting exercise gear', that's one side of the fear ledger. But if a chainsaw-wielding madman were storming through your house, you would not only jog, you would hurdle, parkour, long jump and sprint, all while dialing for the emergency services. (And if anyone did choose to criticise you at this juncture, you would happily use them as an obstacle to slow down the chainsaw-wielding maniac.)

Next time you're quaking in your boots and wishing you had picked up that 'clinical strength' antiperspirant, stop to consider fear not as a barrier to success, but possibly as one of the most overlooked and underutilised motivators we have for driving us to success. Then set about reframing your fear. The trick is to see fear—when appropriate—as a useful tool rather than something to avoid.

APPLYING 'FLIP THE FEAR'

When applying 'Flip the fear', remember the following:

1   Use fear to drive positive outcomes.

2   Define fears so they reflect reality, not wild imagination.

3   Instil appropriate fears around behaviours that need changing.

4   Avoid catastrophising and fear paralysis.

5   Always use fear for action, not inaction.

6   Rebalance your fear so that your desired condition holds less fear than your present situation.

CHAPTER 8

Link it to the known

There are things known and there are things unknown, and in between are the doors of perception.

Aldous Huxley

Any parent who has tried to expand the repertoire of their children's palates has probably unknowingly explored more change-management strategies than the typical human-resources manager at a multinational corporate. There's no nice way to say it: *Change. Simply. Sucks.* And when the change involves the new or unknown, it's downright difficult too.

The remnants of our evolutionary survival instinct—what Seth Godin refers to as the 'lizard' part of our brain—love to flex their muscles whenever something new shows up on the horizon or we feel so rut bound that we decide to strike out in a hitherto unexplored direction (cue: the stomach butterflies). Nonetheless, our fear of the new or the unknown can also have a positive impact on our lives. It exists for a reason, after all.

Arriving home to find the front door ajar with the lock hanging on by a single screw is an unknown that could indicate danger in the form of an intruder—or, it could indicate that a neighbour saw a fire through the window and broke the door down to put it out before it got out of control. What would your first impression be? If you're like most of us, you're programmed to scan the environment for threats a bit more acutely than for opportunities.

But when fear of the unknown skews into the worlds of xenophobia, intolerance and even simple 'stuck-in-the-mudness', it not only costs us as individuals, it costs us all at a community level as well.

Without change—without accepting the risks inherent in any advancement—humanity would be a very sorry lot indeed: poor of health, living a violent hand-to-mouth existence and dying in our thirties with a head bereft of teeth. This is not to say that all change is good, but on average, humanity's capacity to embrace the unknown has been a defining feature of our success.

Fear of the unknown is an almost universal experience, but it is in moving beyond this fear that we achieve more of what we really want in life. In fact, the process of growing up and older is itself an unrelenting journey into the unknown, even though we occasionally meet a few helpful guides along the way who have 'been there' and 'done that' before us.

The truth is, fear of the unknown never really goes away, but it can be faced and its power redirected. Fear of the blank page must be beaten in the pursuit of creativity, fear of unforeseen danger nagging at the back of every explorer's mind must constantly be quelled and every entrepreneur or boot strapping start-up must be willing to take that first step into the unknown in order to realise their vision. There's simply no way around it.

What we tend to do, in a very logical attempt to minimise the risk and ensure we are not completely foolhardy, is conduct research with the aim of reducing the incidence or scale of the unknown. And in fact, some research is an extraordinarily good idea. The problem with this strategy, however, is that it often leads to behaviour best described as, 'ready … aim … aim … aim … aim …' In other words, we become so obsessed with minimising risk that we in fact never move forward (which—although it minimises the risk to zero—is not a particularly helpful strategy).

Most business books will advise you that a more favourable approach may be, 'ready…fire…aim…' But this is easier said than done and doesn't really deal with the issue that's preventing us from pulling the trigger in the first place.

So what drives this fear of the unknown, how do we deal with it, and more importantly, how do we make it work for us?

FAMILIARITY IS JUST SO FAMILIAR

Familiarity wraps us up in a kind of warmth that calms us and makes us feel more at home in a new situation. The irony is that the familiar is not necessarily any safer or more advantageous. Anyone who experienced less than ideal childhood living arrangements can attest to this. But while the familiar may not be any safer, it can act as a sedative and feels more comfortable and oddly reassuring even when it is being impossibly irritating.

Anyone who has ever travelled the world will know the rather odd feeling of relief you encounter when you stumble upon your own accent in a foreign land. People you may pay no attention to under ordinary circumstances come to resemble land in an ocean of unfamiliarity. You instantly feel safer, you confide in these complete strangers as you never would have at home and then you tell yourself the biggest lie of all: 'I must keep in touch with them!'

But this psychological oddity can be an incredibly powerful tool when it comes to motivating yourself, your team or those you wish to have influence with. It enables you to make behavioural change not only more effective, but also more enthusiastic.

It's also one of the reasons why mental rehearsal and guided meditations can be incredibly useful. The more vivid and real the rehearsal feels, the more familiar the real experience will seem once it is undertaken.

It's part of the reason why rehearsal, not just memorising, is important in the creative arts and education. Memorising, like most learning experiences, develops the understanding of a subject at a mental level. Rehearsal embeds the practice in cellular memory. Actors, musicians, comedians and other performers don't rehearse in an effort to become mechanistic in their performances, they rehearse so that their performances feel natural, instinctual and somehow an extension of who they really are.

So, a key strategy to building familiarity with the unknown is to rehearse it until it feels known and familiar. This applies as much to the corporate world of pitching new business and developing critical work skills as it does to educating children and developing productive new habits in ourselves. What this is really about is making the change seem less like change.

One of the most powerful strategies leaders and salespeople can use for making change stick — for helping their teams, families, communities and even themselves adopt positive new behaviours — is to frame them as not new at all. That is, to link them to the known.

So how is the psychological sleight of hand achieved?

One of the great successes of the Marriage Equality Movement was, in fact, its name. It could just as easily have been named the Gay Marriage Movement or the LGBT Marriage Act, which though arguably just as legitimate may have been a harder proposition when it came to garnering popular support.

However, no matter what side of the line you stood on before the idea of 'marriage equality' was proposed, you definitely knew what marriage was and you hopefully had a good understanding of how important equality is. This knowledge was critical for generating the widespread support that the Marriage Equality Movement has enjoyed, even from some surprising sectors of the community. Religious conservatives too saw the power of the language game in play and lobbied hard to have any proposed legislation renamed before it was debated.

By using some of the language and iconography of the civil-rights movements of the 1960s and 1970s, activists linked the idea of marriage equality to racial equality. In other words, they conveyed the idea that this was not something new, but a continuation of a debate that had already been concluded in the affirmative.

Nowhere was this more visible than in the Arizona senate's policy to allow discrimination of service as a religious freedom. This policy asserted that it was a proprietor's right to refuse service to someone they believed was homosexual if they were of a religious faith that outlawed homosexuality.

Critics around the country, and around the world, were quick to point out that the segregation argument had already been had and that rather than this being a policy that supported freedom, it was one that denied essential freedoms to those who were being discriminated against.

This capacity to link the unknown, or at least the misunderstood, to beliefs and practices that are already widely accepted is one of the most persuasive tools a leader, salesperson or even lawmaker has available to them.

This, of course, is not a new skill. The ancient Greeks, Chinese, Indians and Persians all utilised sequential logic thousands of years ago. At each point of their argument they would seduce you into agreeing to its inherent logic before hitting you with an inescapable conclusion that challenged your pre-held beliefs.

Highly persuasive salespeople become deftly skilled at this practice when making an argument for their products or services, building familiarity and minimising perceived risks by pointing out how their product aligns perfectly with what they already believe to be true.

A simplified example of this could be:

1 This is a brand new model of car

2 but it was designed by the same person and firm who designed the car you loved the most in the past

3 therefore, the risk of buying this car is much diminished.

Now this is not an eloquent sales pitch (please never use the phrase, 'Therefore, the risk is much diminished' if you ever hope to make a sale), but it's immediately obvious that the logic is reasonably sound and that something that is unknown—the new model—has been linked to the known, the reliable designer and manufacturer.

What this demonstrates is how fear of the unknown, which really sits at the root of all fears (the acronym False Evidence Appearing Real is rather useful here, although we'd strongly suggest that the word Fantastical would be a more accurate representation of the letter F in this case) can in fact be mitigated or even dismissed by making anything new, different or unexpected seem less so.

SOMETHING LIKE AN ANALOGY

Analogies are one of the primary tools the commercial world thrusts upon us in an effort to shift new products. And when an analogy aligns with our identity and values, it is a heady mix that is hard to resist.

Every great salesperson requires a command of analogy and metaphor and they should use it to create a bridge between their prospect's current position and the sale. Occasionally, the analogy doesn't even have to be spoken or written; it can simply be made by physical placement. At an international car show, Volkswagen decided to secure the stand where Porsche had camped themselves in previous years. The message was clear: 'We've got German engineering just like Porsche … only you can afford us!'

For instance, what do you think of when you read, 'Coco Pops are just like …'? If you were raised in the 1970s or 1980s you immediately complete the phrase in your head, '… a chocolate milkshake, only crunchy'. Advertisers have for decades relied on analogies to make new product lines seem more familiar and therefore less risky.

In fact, this is a tool parents, friends, co-workers, in fact just about all of us, adopt in an effort to entice people to try something new and to make untried experiences seem less of a challenge: 'It's just like riding a bike … or falling off a log … or learning to walk'. We use analogies as a way of linking what's new and possibly threatening to the past and the known.

We use these kinds of analogies all the way through the education process. A lower-case 'd' is like a lower case 'b' only backwards; the 'b', of course, is like a stick and a ball; subtraction is like backwards addition; and spelling is like sounding out a word a little bit at a time.

These associations make it easy for our brains to link up information and to make things more memorable, but most importantly, to make things less of a departure from what we already understand, and that makes them seem easier and more achievable.

Orson Scott Card famously quipped, 'Metaphors have a way of holding the most truth in the least space'. He makes a very good point because it is less important that we know something to be true than it is for us to feel it to be true. In this, metaphors outmuscle even the most studious list of facts and figures, proof points and testimonials. They enable understanding to be both portable and transferable.

What makes the metaphor or analogy so powerful is that it takes truth out of the world of the abstract and places it squarely in our world, our point of reference and ultimately our identity.

This is critical when forming metaphors of your own. There is no point telling someone on a production line that inventory is like advanced mathematics ... unless, of course, they are particularly good at mathematics. It only makes things worse! So, when introducing a new work practice, link it to systems that have previously been used, or to the sports your staff follow or the education they all shared. When driving behavioural change at a cultural level, show how it reflects something that has been done before or aligns with something else they all know to be valuable — something simple and within reach.

LINK IT TO THE PAST

An important strategy for linking to the known is an understanding of the significance of historic precedent. Interestingly, there has been a cultural shift around this principle in the business world in recent times. Where a business with the descriptor, 'Founded in 1873' would have once connoted trust and stability, in modern times it has come to suggest that an organisation may be staid or outdated.

However, even in our modern age we still feel a nostalgia for the past; it's just that the past we feel nostalgic for is a bit more recent, closer to home and more personal. Millennials can be heard pining for 2005: 'Great year that. Time goes by so quickly!'

Such is the power of connections to our past that even the construction of a faux history can be incredibly compelling.

We once consulted on a relaunch in Australia of a soft drink called Kirks. In the 1970s, soft drinks could be delivered in bulk to your door in much the same way as milk could. And although this practice has long since ceased (which, we assume, received much applause from dentists), it is a memory that remained strong in the cultural context of Australia.

The issue around the relaunch was that while Kirks was a brand that was remembered in one state of Australia, all other states had known different brands.

When we were asked to relaunch this product, we were told to target baby boomers and the older members of Gen X, all of whom had grown up in the age of the soft-drink delivery man. We did so by designing a strategy that used a nostalgia for that time — in other words, a recollection of the 1960s to early 1980s — and attributed this nostalgia to Kirks, even though it was not a brand most Australians had grown up with.

The strategy was so effective, and the acceptance of this faux nostalgia so successful (and convincing enough that the team that recorded the jingle for us actually called to ask if it was not just a revival of the original), that the campaign won an Effie Award (a marketing effectiveness award).

This nostalgia for the past is reflected all around the world. Refrigerators designed to look like those we grew up with, even though they are fitted with new technology, remind us of the home we grew up in. Retro-designed furniture, too, although now made from modern fibres and sustainable timber, aligns with a 'simpler' time, or at least a time that we remember through an editorialised memory.

The point is, an ability to frame the new in the past has a way of making the unknown seem much less strange to us.

Another way this manifests is in framing a new experience as something we've seen or done before. Or, failing that, by the suggestion that it's been done before by someone just like you. Any child who endured the constant comparison to older siblings, cousins or 'the child down the street' has more than a passing acquaintance with this strategy.

What this frame enables is for the scale of the change or its impact on us personally to be reduced. As much as workers in the corporate world bemoan change and can be heard to complain, 'not another new system!', the fact that they have changed systems so many times in the past can actually be an asset when trying to remind them of their capacity to make change work.

Again, the strength of this strategy is in its ability to make change seem less like change and, in fact, have it appear as more of what has gone before.

THE LANGUAGE OF CHANGE

It is said that they who control language control the world. This may sound like a trite statement that overstates the power of words, but as any congressperson or senator can attest, words have the power to unseat governments, change laws and shape and drive popular opinion.

Television commentator Bill Maher once observed that when the Republican Party changed the name of the Estate Tax (a tax on the inheritance left by some of the wealthiest individuals in the United States) to Death Tax, popular opinion shifted. 'Death? That could happen to me ... I don't like that tax!'

In fact, political word play, whether it is analogous or euphemistic, has risen to the level where it may now be considered an art. Its use and deployment is a powerful tool that can have us feeling an affinity for a candidate or marching in the street to oppose their policies (assuming, of course, that some wordsmith hasn't renamed 'public assembly' an act of 'civil incitement').

In many ways, the political use of language is simply another way of using logic to make a point. The influence of McCarthyism during the Cold War was predicated on the use of language. At no point did the McCarthyists say they were 'thought policing' or issuing 'state-sanctioned opinions' or enforcing 'Controlled Freedom of Expression'. These concepts were far too Orwellian (and, ironically, Communistic). Instead they campaigned against 'un-American activities'. Which red-blooded American could read those words and object? Not only did the language they used not appear threatening, it also implied that anyone who disagreed with their message might in fact be a threat to the nation and hence those they were trying to engage.

If anything, this example seems too obvious to work, but in the post-war period, the threat of attack from foreign forces still loomed large in the minds of average people.

Today, this subtlety of persuasive language informs corporate communications and drives training and induction processes, graduate selection, education strategies, law and order, foreign policy and just about everything we touch in everyday life. The reason words are so powerful is that language is not merely communication: it is the creation of meaning.

What makes this such an effective strategic tool is that once language has been accepted and culturally absorbed, it is rarely questioned.

Recently, we were brought in to do some work with some exceptional educators and we knew this was a project we could really get behind. This network consists of the teachers, principals, school districts and executives who drive the uptake and availability of technology in schools. Our role was to help them become thought leaders in their industry and community and in doing so help those communities lift their game when it came to technological fluency.

Part of our strategy, as always, was to look at the language being used in the category to identify what value exchange was actually taking place. In other words, what were parents, governments and community leaders really wanting from teachers and schools, beyond words that have become a bit generic, such as 'education', 'skills' and 'results'?

Given the changing nature of technology, it had to be something that could evolve, but just as importantly, the language used had to work as a filter through which future programs and initiatives could be driven without having to add extensions such as 2.0 or 3.0 to maintain relevance.

In the end, we decided to suggest a language palette that was neither education- nor technology-based and to land the language in the values and concerns of parents. What we proffered was that these extraordinary teachers are actually 'future proofing' children. Bringing the language of future proofing children into education was important because not only is it true but it celebrates the importance of what teachers do. In a world of rapid change and exponential demands on teachers and children, they don't only need technology, they also need adaptability, a cognitive agility that enables them to move from platform to platform with a kind of mental flexibility that previous generations, who lived and worked at a gentler pace, did not require. The instant and reflexive response to our reframing of their purpose (and the language around it) was palpable—and the auditorium buzzed.

What we had done was to reframe a fear teachers and parents were all too familiar with: the fear of not keeping up. This encourages a shift in society's view of teaching from imparting information to mentoring and development, and in doing so raises the value of teachers in their own eyes as well as making them thought leaders in their communities.

PERCEPTION IS EVERYTHING

Okay, clearly the statement that perception is everything is palpably a lie, but like all good lies, it has a truth poking through it. That 'truth' is that although fear of the unknown may be a misplaced fear, and all the known evidence points towards it being an irrational fear, as we have already asserted, fear is one of the most powerful motivators that exists.

So, by accepting this and the fact that fears are a part of human psychology—at least for the foreseeable (or unknown) future—we think it is astute to work with our fears and turn them into assets.

When Kieran's little girl got a splinter in her foot it was as though the world was going to end. Tears were flowing and shrieks were heard streets away. Kieran held her frightened little girl while her husband held a little foot in one hand and tweezers in the other. Meanwhile, a small voice dripping with betrayal screamed, 'No ... no ... no, Daddy!' In seconds, Daddy had removed the splinter, but the crying didn't stop. It continued unabated until Kieran soothed her little girl by saying, 'It's gone, darling'. The screaming stopped in an instant and Darcy sprang up with a quizzical expression on her face and looked at her foot wondering what all the fuss had been about.

It can be like that in business too. Consider the fear around the supposed demise of cinema. With every advance in technology or new competitor into the sector the doomsayers chanted: 'Cinema will die! Cinema will die!' First it was television, then VHS players appeared in every home, then we all got DVDs and now we have access to instant downloads. But cinema has not died. People still love going to the movies. The point is, cinema is not just about the movie you are watching, it is about going out, holding hands and sharing the fear or joy or elation while we watch stories bigger than ourselves (figuratively and literally). Again, the perceived fear exceeds the eventual reality.

The same may prove true with regard to the fears surrounding the future of shopping malls in a world of online shopping. While some concern may be warranted, perhaps a different perspective, such as digging into what they truly offer beyond simply selling stuff you often don't need anyway, is what's necessary in order to survive and thrive.

So it is with all fear. We project into a future we don't really understand and assume the worst, even if we don't know precisely what the worst is. All progress — all advancement, creativity, productiveness and performance — is a result of us facing such fears and using them to propel us forward.

This is what Think Scared truly means. It is not an instruction to live our lives in fear, which is in some ways the assumption because fear is always with us. What we mean is that, rather than ignoring fear, trying to hide it or from it, or simply pretending that it doesn't exist, we should all learn to use it.

The martial arts famously take energy that is aimed at them as an attack and redirect this energy towards their own objectives. In doing so, a smaller artist is able to defeat a much larger combatant. So it is with fear. Fear of loss is more powerful than gain as a motivator for most of us. Although we try to define ourselves outwardly as driven more by positivity than negativity, our behaviour—what we do as opposed to what we say—begs to differ.

So, instead of indulging in a fantasy about how we would like to imagine we are, we may all be better served by accepting how we are wired and, instead, use this to our advantage.

APPLYING 'LINK IT TO THE KNOWN'

When applying 'Link it to the known', remember the following:

1 Rehearse critical behaviours to make them more familiar.

2 Make the change seem less like change.

3 Use analogies to create links to precedent.

4 Demonstrate how new behaviours are like older, well-understood behaviours.

5 Change the language you use around change to shift the emotional response.

CHAPTER 9

Show them they're not alone

Nothing brings you together like a common enemy.

David Foster Wallace

Social isolation is well documented by social psychologists as detrimental to our mental health, but it seems it is damaging for us physically as well—and not merely in the sense that we stop shaving and using deodorant.

WE ARE A SOCIAL SPECIES

It turns out isolation can be a real problem. An alarming study of those most likely to be alone, the socially isolated elderly, found a 26 per cent increase in their mortality rates. The 2010 study, conducted by the US-based organisation AARP, found too much alone time could be just as bad as smoking 15 cigarettes a day.

There is also growing dissatisfaction with the way many prison systems use isolation as punishment. The concept of solitary confinement was introduced into US prisons in the early nineteenth century, but was quickly abandoned as the effects on the prisoners were so evidently negative. It was concluded that solitary confinement sent people mad. Today it has been reintroduced, with its defenders asserting that it is no longer the solitary it once was. (The spaces are no longer dark holes, they say, because although they are still windowless, they are rather well lit little boxes.) The effects, however, are believed by many to ultimately be the same.

Scientists and psychologists have discovered numerous negative effects of solitary confinement, such as constant and heightened anxiety, headaches, lethargy, heart palpitations, depression, insomnia, nightmares, fear of impending nervous breakdown and in some cases suicidal thoughts. The UN has even concluded that it is a form of torture.

Juan E. Méndez, United Nations Special Rapporteur on Torture and Other Cruel, Inhuman and Degrading Treatment or Punishment (now there's a title for a business card!) concluded that, 'Segregation, isolation, separation, cellular lockdown, Supermax, the hole, Secure Housing Unit…whatever the name, solitary confinement should be banned by States as a punishment or extortion technique'. He said that even 15 days of isolation can cause psychological damage, making it a form of torture, and called for it to be banned in the vast majority of cases.

The primary reason why it is so damaging is because of the social isolation it creates. It stops people from having the meaningful and vital social interactions they long for and need. It appears loneliness is among the top-10 fears of human beings for good reason: it can cause us deep psychological damage. Besides, none of us wants to be Bridget Jones…eating ice-cream from a tub and playing Celine Dion's 'All by myself' over and over again.

Isolation is psychologically damaging to us because we are fundamentally social creatures. (Some experts believe this is tied to an unconscious panic that mimics the fear once felt by primitive humans when they were left alone, without a social unit, to fend off wild animals and danger — in other words, to find themselves the only lunch item on the menu.)

Our emotional minds are wired for social connections. Neural resonance is said to take place in our brains as they come to be in sync with each other. This is believed to help us connect with others. When it happens, it reduces barriers and increases empathy. It helps us work together better.

What's more, the sociability of human beings helped our societies blossom as collaboration increased and large-scale cooperation emerged. Tribes, remote villages, towns, large cities—in fact, the entire planet—are all collaborative structures. Working cooperatively and interconnectedly has contributed to human beings thriving as a species. It has helped us move from a nomadic existence to become settlers. It has produced culture and agriculture, built countless companies and businesses, and brought with it great technological development.

Alone humankind wandered; together we thrived.

SOCIAL MEDIA EXISTS FOR A REASON

We are continually bombarded with extraordinary facts about social-networking platforms and today will be no exception.

There are presently more than 1.15 billion Facebook users, which means if Facebook were a country it would be more populous than China. There are 58 billion tweets per day, or 9100 tweets per second; 91 per cent of smartphone internet access is for social activities; and online social activity is still the number-one internet activity, beating out even porn (apparently, today we really do just want to be friends).

As intrinsically interesting as this is, we are more fascinated by why this has occurred. What compels human beings en masse to share their lives, ideas, beliefs, feelings, selfies and images of what they had for breakfast? (Incidentally, Dan has an unfriending policy for those who share photos of what they ate for lunch. One photo of an amazing seared tuna and you are in immediate danger of being 'unfriended'.)

What drives us to share and even over-share? (On that subject, we think Facebook could do with an extra button or two. 'Like' could be augmented by 'overshare' and a button for whenever 'like' seems rather callous and ill-timed. It always feels a bit odd to read about a friend's pet dying, and then hitting the word 'like'—just something for you to consider, Mr Zuckerberg.)

The 'Why?', it transpires, is rather simple. We value connection. We are social creatures compelled by our evolution to connect and relate to each other. Science is beginning to document the wiring of our social brain as neural scanners map our emotional responses to social stimuli. In his book *Social: Why Our Brains are Wired to Connect*, neuroscientist Matthew D. Lieberman argues that we are designed to seek social connection. He writes, 'These adaptations intensify the bonds we feel with those around us and increase our capacity to predict what is going on in the minds of others so that we can better coordinate and cooperate with them'.

THERE IS SAFETY IN NUMBERS

Numbers give us a sense of safety and even courage.

When you are afraid, one of the last things you want is to be ... alone! The horror movie genre has mastered the art of manipulating this fear. No-one wants to be that girl in the horror movie who inexplicably runs away from the safety of a crowd towards the darkest, most vacant and obviously dangerous part of the house or forest. For many of us, our level of anxiety still increases when we are alone and in the dark, even as adults.

The logic for this is rather obvious: numbers typically reduce risk. The crazy man in the ice-hockey mask has much less chance of turning us into human minced meat when we are in a pack than as a solo combatant running on our own.

Revealing the numbers is also an excellent way of delivering a tricky or slightly embarrassing message. For this reason it is a strategy frequently employed by drug companies, government departments and those with messages relating to social issues from herpes, to depression and anxiety, fungal infections to thrush, weight problems, money issues, gambling addictions and other social maladies. All of these attempt to make us feel, if not safe, in sufficient company not to panic by demonstrating we are part of a larger group with phrases such as, '9 out of 10 recommend...', '1 in 3 experience...' and 'The average woman/man/child...'

Numbers have a way of reducing the social risk too. The question is this: how do you make them meaningful? How do you stop them being just another statistic? When you add meaning to numbers, magic can happen.

THE DESIRE TO BE 'NORMAL'

People ultimately just want to feel normal. Now don't get this confused with average. We want to feel special, not average, but we also want to be normal rather than a 'freak'. By normalising things that may seem to deviate from the accepted norm or as potentially odd or simply different, we remove barriers and we subsequently reduce isolation.

ABC's *Modern Family* is a global television hit, having amassed millions of viewers and multiple Emmy Awards. It is funny and endearing, but its real power lies in making us feel less alone, less of an oddball.

Traditionally, families portrayed on television have been both whole in the nuclear family sense and wholesome in the moral sense of their era. As time passed and our societies evolved, it was a bit alienating as we struggled to reconcile our crazy lives with those idealistic lives being played back to us on our television screens.

However, *Modern Family* does not operate this way. Instead, it normalises crazy, mixed-up families that feel more like ours, or at least as varied as ours, so we begin to accept a more flexible model of 'family'. For most of us the show is not a mirror—statistically the majority of children are not raised by gay parents—but it still represents universal insights into the trials and tribulations of keeping a family unit functional in this modern world.

Ty Burrell, who plays Phil Dunphy in *Modern Family* is well aware of the progress the show has made at a cultural level.

'It's one of my favourite things about the show. I love it when I talk to conservatives and they're describing all three couples, and they never mention that one of them is gay. That's the brilliance of the writing. In a completely unaggressive, apolitical way, they are showing this couple as completely normal, dealing with ordinary stuff...'

By normalising each of the families, their values and challenges, we connect their experience to the rest of us.

Clubs and sub-cultures have worked along these principles for a long time. In isolation, being a grown man who collects Star Wars toys and leaves them in their boxes, refusing to let children even touch them, may be considered a bit odd. But as part of a club or at a convention of Star Wars aficionados you are not only normal, you may even be considered cool.

These demonstrations that we are not alone can have a profound effect on human behaviour and engagement. Public Health England, a government initiative in the UK, successfully employed this strategy to get teens to have uncomfortable conversations via their Awkward Conversations campaign.

They asked ChannelFlip's YouTube bloggers to create videos on awkward conversations about sex, drugs and alcohol and watched as the personal comments rolled in and the conversations flowed. The message was clear: you may be awkward, but you are not alone.

Human beings may not wish to be described as common but we are reassured by our commonality. As a leader, an organisation, a brand or an individual, it is often useful to consider and celebrate the commonalities and to align them with our behaviour.

HELP US 'FIT IN'

There is much written about how 'different' teenagers are today, and in many ways they have been exposed to very different stimuli during their upbringing from those of previous generations. The flipside of this is that, in many ways, nothing has changed.

It's almost become comedic to hear a new generation bemoan how 'different' they are. Yes, we get it, 'you're all individuals together!' However, the current generations of Millennials, Gen Zs and the like have had the internet from birth so they truly have been exposed to more ideas than any generation before them. As a consequence they will not follow the herd. Actually, having said this, even the herd is not following the herd; there are actually lots of herds to follow these days.

You only need to look at a group of teens to see they, like all teens before them, are still much defined by not doing what their parents did. In an effort to define themselves, fads pass through them like wildfire: Gangnam, photo bombing, planking, twerking and sellotape selfies (seriously?).

However, the truth is that 'social leprosy' is as much a fear for them as it is for any generation before them. In fact, it is a fear for most human beings. Rejection hurts. Just the idea of it can make us flinch, literally.

Those au fait with the work of leading social neuroscience researcher at UCLA Naomi Eisenberger may recall her experiment where subjects played a computer game called Cyberball. The game consisted of two virtual players and a person (the subject) throwing the ball among themselves. Halfway through the game the two virtual players started throwing the ball to each other only, leaving out the subject completely. While this was transpiring, Eisenberger mapped the brain activity of the now excluded player and discovered that the part of the brain that lit up was the same part that reacts to physical pain (the dorsal part of the anterior cingulate cortex, for those who enjoy their Latin).

Social rejection hurts, whereas great engagement makes people feel included. Inclusive organisations are the ones paving the way for the future. It is important to remember this when dealing with disengaged staff. Often they are disengaged because they do not feel included in the first place. Keep your friends close and your staff closer!

However, social exclusion can also be a powerful motivator for discouraging unwanted behaviours. In Australia, as in most developed nations, the greatest incidence of fatalities involving motor vehicles occurs among young men. In an effort to stem this tide, roads and transport authorities ran campaign after shockingly graphic campaign driving home the message, 'If you speed you will die'. Occasionally the message was expanded to suggest that you may also kill your friends.

And yet, the incidence of speeding among young men continued to increase. Subsequent research revealed that young people—men in particular—are so far removed from any experience of death, they consider themselves invincible. In other words, they cannot even conceive of their own demise. What they can imagine, however, with quite a lot of emotional intensity, is 'social death'.

The ensuing campaign, created by Clemenger BBDO, to dissuade young speeding drivers featured women looking at the young men and judging them by raising a pinky finger. The warning read, 'Speeding. No-one thinks big of you', a message that bypassed the logical and went straight for the … well … the most vulnerable part of a man's psyche.

The global hit 'Dumb ways to die', created in Australia by McCann, uses a similar strategy. Simply put, it says getting hit by a train is a stupid way to die: as dumb as setting fire to your hair or poking a grizzly bear with a stick.

CONNECT US TO EACH OTHER

An important factor in showing us we are not alone, particularly in the social media age, is to connect us to each other. This also demonstrates how important connectivity and teamwork are to success.

The myth of solo success is all-pervasive. Although we love tales of the lone hero battling the odds, facing the enemy alone, rising in solitary defiance of the challenges they encounter before savouring the sweet victory of having done it all themselves, the reality is far from it. Even the Lone Ranger had help. Lone? Seriously? What about Silver? And Tonto? He's standing right next to him in all the posters (how very insulting).

Every hero has help. Consider the Olympic athlete. Behind every Olympian is a massive team: coaches, trainers, masseuses, psychologists, training partners, equipment providers, sponsors, government grants, statisticians and camera operators. The average price of an Olympic gold medal runs well into seven figures for most events.

Success is not a solo pursuit; it is more likely to happen when we work together.

Crowd sourcing is rapidly becoming a critical tool for connecting us to each other and to business. Communities are now willing and able to co-create your brand and business with you. Kickstarter (kickstarter.com) famously crowd sources funding for new ideas; Starbucks crowd sources and co-creates new product ideas and even store design through My Starbucks Idea (www.mystarbucksidea.com); and NASA recently crowd sourced designs for a new spacesuit.

But our focus should be on more than simply crowd sourcing. It is actually crowd connecting: attracting like minds and building shared language and goals. An ability to connect each of us to one other is becoming the killer app in this collaborative era.

CONNECT US TO SOMETHING BIGGER THAN OURSELVES

Human beings also feel less alone and isolated when they are connected to a cause that is bigger than anything they could achieve on their own. When we worked with Coca-Cola, it was fascinating to see how desperate consumers were for Coca-Cola to behave like a big brand. Despite all of the criticism levelled at Coke from different sectors, people didn't want them to behave smaller. They wanted them to use their scale to do something meaningful and large.

This is not really so surprising. 'Coke' is famously the second most recognised word around the globe, after 'okay', and as long as Coca-Cola has that kind of power, people expect it to be used for something worthwhile. Our favourite work from Coke came out of the Philippines. As it turns out, in the Philippines people often leave their families and move to other countries where they can earn enough money to support their families back home, often for years at a time. All of the money they make is sent home and they can't afford the cost of travel to visit the very people they are supporting. Coke's brand is all about creating connections and social enjoyment so they created a campaign to help these people visit their loved ones (cut to tear rolling down Kieran's cheek)

133

where the prizes were trips home caught on film by accompanying camera crews.

This 'social imperative' affects the decisions we make and how we spend our time.

What people love about movies and films is seeing them with an audience. (There's a big difference between the two, by the way. A movie is something that has popular success. Often lines from films will be adopted into our vernacular, 'I'll be back'. A film is art and is typically viewed by seven people — including the director … and their mum.) Seeing the way an audience collectively laughs or cries or cringes or shares a fright is a powerful experience. When you watch a movie in a cinema you are not alone — you are part of a bigger and deeper experience.

Organisations that are able to harness the desire of people to connect can build scale on the back of those connections. One Water funds clean-water projects in Africa with every bottle that is bought. Retailer Tom's Shoes donates a pair of shoes to someone in need for every pair it sells in store. Nike's Chalkbot enabled spectators to leave chalk messages of support on the streets of France during the Tour de France and Speight's, a beer brand in New Zealand, enlisted the entire Kiwi population to help send a traditional Kiwi alehouse around the world on a ship so that Kiwi expats living in London could drink a proper New Zealand beer.

All of these organisations and products connected people to something bigger, something they would not be capable of achieving on their own.

WATCH OUR SIX

Feeling that you are not alone is akin to knowing someone else is watching your back. There is a sense of solidarity, an intangible feeling of support. Workplaces and brands that 'have our backs' are more and more those we seek to spend our time and money with.

An example from the cut-throat world of financial services is American Express. In the modern finance industry, organisations struggle to stand for something greater than greed. Their customers, similarly, are questioning what they truly value as the marketplace moves towards less conspicuous consumption. So what do you do when you *are* the money guys—when you are the company that can be accused (and often is accused) of encouraging people to spend money they do not have?

If you're American Express, you create Small Business Saturday, a day when Americans are asked to support their local businesses.

Not only does this demonstrate to small business owners that they're not alone, it goes some way to assuring them that someone in the corporate world has their back, even if they do get something out of it themselves.

So whose back have you got?

SHOW US THE LOVE

Always remember that every exchange, commercial or personal, is a chance to build a relationship. Today, no matter what we do, we are all in the business of relationships and many of the rules that apply to personal relationships translate to the business world too.

For example, we all know one of the cardinal rules of dating is not to talk incessantly about yourself: 'Let me tell you why you should like me', 'Let me tell you how wonderful I am'. It's a dating no no. It's annoying. It's off-putting. We walk away, phone our friends and say 'what an egomaniac'. Yet too often that's exactly how business behaves (it's almost as if we're driven by selfishness—imagine that!).

Businesses and salespeople need to learn how to love their customers—to let them talk about their feelings and be genuinely interested in them. If you see a customer merely as a dollar sign, or your staff as replaceable, you won't keep them very long because someone else will see them as people worth building relationships with.

The best leaders don't try to dominate. The best salespeople don't try to coerce you; they build trust and they nurture relationships.

Consider the service of Morton's The Steakhouse. Peter Shankman of Shankman Honig was waiting for a flight to Newark and he was hungry. So he tweeted Morton's: '... I'm hungry. Meet me at Newark with a steak'. When he landed at Newark, he found a gentleman in a tuxedo with a Morton's steak and some mashed potato waiting for him. Peter Shankman knows he's not alone!

Ask yourself what kind of relationship your staff and customers have with your organisation. Is it in good shape? Do they feel listened to? Connected? Or do they feel alone?

How are you going to show them they are not alone and that you will be the best relationship they ever had?

APPLYING 'SHOW THEM THEY'RE NOT ALONE'

When applying 'Show them they're not alone', remember the following:

1 There is safety in numbers so make those numbers visible to us.

2 Normalise preferred behaviours through exposure to them.

3 Create channels for us to join and feel like we fit into, as if we were 'members'.

4 Connect us to each other. Build communities of common ground.

5 Connect us to something bigger than we could be on our own.

6 Have our back.

7 Show us the love.

PART IV
Think stupid

This may sound like an oxymoron. Can you actually Think Stupid? Does thinking not by its very nature make us more intelligent? We believe you can in fact Think Stupid and that you must if you are to master human behaviour and wield influence. Thinking Stupid is fundamentally about three things.

Make it simple
How can we construct the least complicated process with the fewest steps, well-understood communications and instructions using only an essential number of hands to achieve our goals?

Make it easy (lazy)
How can we achieve what we want without the need for high involvement? In other words, what are the behavioural shortcuts that could be employed to enable success?

Make it hard not to
How can we create barriers to undesired behaviours, while moving preferred behaviours and rituals closer in terms of proximity and availability?

CHAPTER 10

Make it simple

*If you can't explain it to a six year old,
you don't understand it yourself.*

Einstein

To be perfectly honest, writing an entire chapter on the importance of simplicity does seem something of an oxymoron. As a small measure of acknowledgement to this contradiction, we have included this simplified cheat sheet of shortcuts.

MAKE-IT-SIMPLE SHORTCUTS

1 We are already ridiculously busy and overloaded with information, so make things easy to digest and simple to action.

2 If you make our lives more complicated, we will simply ignore you.

3 We have more options than we need, so make yours simple to understand.

4 If you can't fit it onto a post-it or explain it to a six year old, it needs simplifying.

(continued)

MAKE-IT-SIMPLE SHORTCUTS *(cont'd)*

5   Identify the most basic need or value you need to satisfy and start there.

6   Information curators are the new power brokers.

If, however, you wish to delve a little deeper into the complicated world of simplicity, please read on.

CONFUSION PARALYSES US

We adore the term 'analysis paralysis'. It truly captures the indecision that arises when simplicity is absent and complexity reigns. Today we really can, and frequently do, know too much. In this age of information overload, the famous quote by legendary martial artist Bruce Lee hits the nail squarely on the head: 'If you spend too much time thinking about a thing, you'll never get it done'.

Where once holding knowledge, especially secret knowledge, gave you power, in the age of Google and WikiLeaks information is now infinitely available, so much so that it frequently renders us powerless and gripped by procrastination and indecision.

When basic becomes complicated

It is remarkably easy to become lost in a sea of options, possibilities and opposing views. Consider how difficult it is for new parents to buy an essential such as a baby carriage — or is it a pram, a buggy, a push chair or a stroller? Just getting the name right is enough to send most young mothers and fathers into a panic.

Most people who have not been through the process presume this is a relatively simple matter. Certainly people have been wheeling babies around now for more than a century. And so, once you have peed on the little plastic stick and determined you are indeed pregnant, and have shared the news with your loved ones, you head down to the nearest baby superstore to stock up on the various baby-related products you require and resolve to choose a stroller that matches both your style and budget, which should leave ample time for a walk, reading the newspaper and a cup of frothy coffee.

Of course, that's not what happens at all. Today the majority of new parents, particularly mothers, experience a completely different process.

For starters, having learned you are pregnant, you first have to debate whether or not you should find out the sex of the baby so you can accessorise accordingly. And it's not a simple matter of blue and pink as it once was. (That would be much too old fashioned and likely to scar the youngster with the stain of gender stereotyping right from the get go.)

Better make a list!

Thankfully, there is now laptop and tablet technology that enables you to create spreadsheets where you can prepare to compare the essentials of life with a newborn in the house. So you place parent-propelled transport right up near the top of the list. Next, you ask a few friends for advice, only to discover that their opinions vary wildly so you decide you need to do some research of your own.

You spend hours online researching and reading countless reviews on baby carriage sites, stroller blogs and consumer protection social pages with names made from puns so bad that they would make a hairdressing salon wince.

Once you venture into a store, all of the confidence you had in your research evaporates as you try, unsuccessfully, to fold and unfold one or two strollers, become bamboozled by issues you had not considered—such as aerodynamics, sizes and weights—and return home sans stroller.

You research some more, discover there is a service called Strollerqueen that reviews strollers for you and that, for a fee, will email you advice customised to your needs. By this stage, you are so desperate and hormonally driven you decide to pay for this information because your partner is reaching the limit of their patience and is desperately resisting the urge to scream, 'Just pick one!' This usually manifests as a rather insincere, 'whichever one you want darling', but you decide to *pretend* the two statements don't mean exactly the same thing and press on.

At last you do make your decision and purchase your baby transporting device, usually one that is much more expensive than the average mattress, which, by comparison, has a much longer lifespan than your stroller.

But you're not done yet. The baby arrives and you use your stroller, defend it and discuss its merits with other mothers to the point of exhaustion. Then, some weeks later, your realise what you really need is a small, light, cheap stroller for quick trips to the store because the large, technologically advanced 'Baby RV' you bought weighs significantly more than it did in the store and now occupies the entire boot of the sensible people mover you bought (because that's what new mums drive, isn't it?)

You whip down to one of the less expensive department stores, pick up a cheap stroller—or buy one second hand on eBay—storing the 'Baby RV' away to gather dust. (This scenario may or may not be based on Kieran's personal experience as she is too embarrassed to own up to how a smart woman could become so paralysed and indecisive about buying a stroller.)

As the perceived significance and pressure of the decision amplifies, so does the paralysis. It's not hard to see why so many boards and executive teams of organisations spend countless hours debating, researching and considering options and then fail to reach a resolution, or why employees act like deer in headlights just trying to do the right thing.

Simplicity, it seems, is less simple than it sounds.

Choice isn't always freedom

A typical supermarket in the modern world holds more than 47 000 products on its shelves. Only 30 years ago, that number was closer to 9000. Crest alone has more than 50 types of toothpaste—that's more kinds of toothpaste from a single producer than we have teeth in even the healthiest of mouths.

And if it's confusing for customers, consider how hard it is for the manufacturer. The consumer really only has a few dollars at stake in their toothpaste-buying dilemma, but when you're a production line with more than 50 types of a single product to manufacture, a single commercial misstep could cost you millions of dollars, the loyalty of customers and even the jobs of your colleagues (or yours, for that matter).

Questions become a sort of torture: Which products do you delete? Which do you keep? Which represent the essence of who you are as an organisation? Will your competitors make a land grab for shelf space? Will your customers stick, or switch to another variant you own or to one of your competitors? And this is just one of the 47 000 lines in your supermarket!

It's worth remembering that simplicity and clarity go hand in glove, and the reason both are so valuable is that clarity gives us the freedom to act. We make better decisions, our staff feel more empowered, our children know where the line is drawn and our customers know what we stand for and what to expect from us. When you have clarity and seek simplicity, decisions such as these become easier, and in fact, may help you avoid such a complicated product proliferation in the first place.

The art of simplicity

Apple is the poster child for the power of clarity and simplicity and it has only 60 or so products on offer. So simple was Apple's vision, that it enabled 'cool' to be defined by a guy in a black turtle-neck. Steve Jobs was a passionate advocate of simplicity: 'That's been one of my mantras—focus and simplicity. Simple can be harder than complex: You have to work hard to get your thinking clean to make it simple. But it's worth it in the end, because once you get there, you can move mountains'.

Jonathan Ive, Apple's head of design, admits that Apple's simplicity isn't as simple as it looks, adding, 'True simplicity is derived from so much more than just the absence of clutter and ornamentation. It's about bringing order to complexity'.

Very Zen. But if simple is so cool, why does complexity get to act so superior?

COMPLEXITY DOESN'T EQUAL INTELLIGENCE

Our academic pursuits, right from our first days at school, seem to have a corrupting influence on our attitude to simplicity. Being 'simple' is often used as a term of disrespect to indicate unintelligence or dim-wittedness.

We frequently suffer from the misconception that if we understand something complicated, or use contextual language that the majority of the population cannot understand, we are somehow intellectually superior. This may be the case, although those who fully grasp a concept tend to be able to understand it well enough to make themselves understood (a sentiment echoed by Mr Einstein at the opening of this chapter).

We carry this belief into our everyday lives and workplaces driven by the need to demonstrate our cleverness and value and hopefully avoid being thought of as unsophisticated.

Corporate warriors constantly mistake volume for evidence of both industry and the robustness of their thinking, adding copious charts, graphs and slides where a well-worded statement would suffice.

'Death by PowerPoint' is rather an appropriate term for what transpires every day in many of the world's boardrooms—every bullet point, every Venn diagram or fancy transition steals time from our lives that we never get back.

Complexity is abused and overused all around us. In fact, according to Chris Zook from Bain & Company about 85 per cent of executives he interviewed felt the biggest barrier to sustained profit was not a lack of opportunity but rather that it was related to the internal complexity of their organisations and the management of their energy against this complexity.

Bain & Company spent years researching the causes of enduring profit and success. In Chris Zook's words, 'We found an increasing premium to simplicity in the world of today — not just simplicity of organization, but more fundamentally to an essential simplicity at the heart of strategy itself. In every industry, we discovered companies that were enjoying an inherent advantage in dealing with the increasing tension of faster moving markets and increased internal complexity due to this ability to keep things simpler and more transparent than their rivals'.

So, what Chris Zook and Bain & Company are really getting at is, 'Complex bad, simple good'. Got it? Good.

Simplicity is about distillation. It requires losing superfluous layers, prioritising, letting go and ultimately working out what is fundamental. It was Mark Twain who penned one of the most insightful notes on simplicity when he wrote that he was sorry about writing such long letter but he did not have the time to write a short one.

Most of us neither make the time nor develop the clarity to simplify our thinking. We are all 'writing long letters', if you will, a habit we must break if we are to be more nimble and effective in a world of change.

WE'RE TUNING OUT AND TURNING OFF

Today we are subjected to more information than ever before. According to the University of California in San Diego, in 2008 the average household in the United States consumed a staggering 3.6 zettabytes of data every single year. How much is 3.6 zettabytes, you say? To give you some analogous context, it is the equivalent of reading 174 newspapers, 10845 trillion words or more than 16 average-sized hard drives of information ... every day!

The typical American spends an average of 12 hours a day absorbing content. Consider that these figures date from 2008, so by the time you read this book, it will have increased markedly. Smartphone usage — still a relatively new addition to how we consume information and entertainment — now accounts for two hours a day. Suffice to say our greymatter is getting rather busy. We refer to this state as 'unintentional misdirection'.

Magicians traditionally employ what Gustav Kuhn from the University of Durham classifies as the tactic of misdirection. The theory is to occupy the eyeballs and attention of the audience so they stop noticing what is going on elsewhere.

You may remember an experiment by two psychologists, Daniel Simons and Christopher Chabris, in which subjects are asked to watch a film and try to count how many passes of a basketball are made by the people on screen while a man in a gorilla suit walks in among them. Most people fail to see the gorilla because they are so preoccupied with the task they were given. When the film is played to the subjects again and the gorilla is pointed out, most struggle to believe that this is the same piece of film they originally witnessed.

This is what happens to our attention every day. We are constantly in a state of unintentional misdirection because our overloaded minds are actually looking to edit out information, not add more in. This is why simplicity is so vital. If something comes across as too complicated, not only may we not bother to engage, we may not even notice it in the first place.

Even entertaining videos on YouTube reach a point of attention decay incredibly quickly. Wisitia video tracking asserts that when a video is only 30 seconds in length, 85 per cent of viewers watch it to the end. Compare this to only 50 per cent for videos of between two and four minutes.

Perhaps this is because we are less likely to be distracted in 30 seconds than over a period of minutes, but it may also be due to the fact that we have been conditioned by 30-second commercials and 20-second news stories in mainstream media. Whatever the case may be, shorter, simpler pieces of communication are more likely to drive attention and clarity of message.

Where simplicity is absent, it is far easier to turn your attention elsewhere, and as we have established, people generally prefer this route.

We believe this is one of the greatest challenges when it comes to the 'green' message. Our planet is in a state of unprecedented crisis, yet radical action has failed to transpire. It is just too confusing, too complicated and too hard. Competing messages abound, as do thousands upon thousands of strategies. Government and experts argue at countless meetings and summits and the rest of the world resigns itself to the fact that if the experts cannot agree, how can we know what to do. We simply avert our attention.

Yet we are all happy to do something simple, such as turning our lights off once a year for Earth Hour. Although we're not defending Earth Hour, its true purpose of changing public awareness and policy has been rather effective. What we do wish to point out is that people are willing to engage and act when they are given clear and simple messages and options.

Food and diet suffer from the same issue. People are so confused by the plethora of messages and 'doctor-endorsed' diets that many are simply tuning out and giving up. In research groups and reports we constantly hear people express that they don't know what to eat anymore. Every week there is a new food we simply must eat because it has superpowers; a food we should avoid that causes all kinds of unfortunate side effects; and something that is in fashion and out of fashion. Then there are food miles, high protein, low GI, carbo-loading, carb-free, low fat, low sugar, low calorie ...

We don't have an obesity problem so much as a clarity problem. We can't keep up. What to eat has become so confusing that many people are afraid of food and eating. This is a tragedy. Something so essential to our survival — something that provides much of life's pleasure and that gathers us together — is now to be feared because something very simple has been made impossibly complicated.

TOO HARD IS JUST TOO HARD

With all the choice we enjoy today, if it's too complicated, people simply won't bother. The 'too-hard basket' may be a cliché, but it is full to overflowing.

Once upon a time, life was much less complicated. Those days are now long gone, but so too is our patience for convoluted processes.

Today, we simply seek another option...and Google is happy to provide millions in mere moments.

What we need is information curation.

CURATORS NEEDED!

The growth of information and complexity means the ability to simplify is desperately needed. And this is something that also has immense commercial value.

To make it through the jungle of options out there we're turning to those who can cut to the important information and simply connect us to the things we need to know. Curators are the tour guides of the information age. They are today much more than just simplifiers, they are the true power brokers.

There are three primary types of curation at play:

- curation by collaboration
- curation by information
- curation by reputation.

Curation by collaboration

Technology has made this type of curation both possible and powerful. It involves gathering the opinions of communities and filtering information and content. Sites such as TripAdvisor (www. tripadvisor.com.au) are wonderful examples of this type of curation. The community is responsible for uploading reviews and even photographs and video of their experiences, turning each individual into an exhibitor whose contribution is then curated by the collective. TripAdvisor is now a more trusted source than most travel agents.

Of course, there's also mega community curators such as Facebook, which enable users to share their music favourites and recommendations with friends via Spotify. Even YouTube serves us content curated by the community based on the number of views a video has received, enabling us to navigate the exabytes of information available to us.

Curation by information

This type of curation relies on statistics to predict content that will appeal to us. By gathering information about the preferences of people just like us, these information curators are able to serve up relevant content, making it simple for us to find things we like. It is fascinating that this kind of curation not only filters information, it now also drives, and arguably simplifies, the creation of content that will statistically appeal to viewers.

The streaming service Netflix has already successfully used data to commission David Fincher to produce the hit series *House of Cards*. The hit 2013 series was not piloted or researched but rather based on information gathered from the two billion hours of content consumed by its users each month.

Netflix's Todd Yellin says of the process he designed, 'We climb under the hood and get all greasy with algorithms, numbers and vast amounts of data. Getting to know users, millions of them, and what they play. If they play one title, what did they play after, before, what did they abandon after five minutes?' This process involves big data. Interestingly the goal of this information capture is ultimately simple, to inform Netflix on how to serve us more content we will love.

Curation by reputation

The third type of curation relies on profile and trust. This can come from celebrity, brand or time spent earning your stripes. Celebrity curation is, and will continue to be, a powerhouse in the curation world. Once upon a time, before celebrities ruled magazine covers, it was models who drove what we wore and desired. Today celebrities are the stars we navigate our lives by.

Reputation is a powerful curator. Today the majority of blockbusters are built on reputations and franchises; they are the sequels. In 1981 only two sequels made the top-10 box office list for the year (incidentally they were *Superman II* and the Bond movie *For Your Eyes Only*). In 2011 that number was a staggering eight. So it seems even Hollywood is getting into the curation business.

The future belongs to those who can serve us just the portions we require and desire. And that will require some simplification.

WILL IT FIT ON A POST-IT NOTE?

3M's Post-it Notes are one of our favourite tools for keeping life simple.

We have a rule when developing the briefs we write for the organisations we work with: if it doesn't fit onto a single Post-it Note and it can't be read from a distance, you have not clarified your thinking simply enough (just so we're clear, we're referring to the original Post-it Notes, not large conference flip charts). When you simplify things down to a single Post-it Note you get the clearest, most effective and most enjoyable communication.

Most organisations have vision and mission statements that take up an entire wall—far from the simple Post-it Note square—whereas companies with memorable missions have applied the discipline of simplicity. Here are a few of our favourites.

- Tesla. Make electric cars awesome.
- The Body Shop. Beauty that isn't ugly.
- Nike. The heroism of participation.
- Axe. Punch above your weight.

TAKE THE 'SIX-YEAR-OLD' TEST

Once you have clarified and simplified there is one last torture test needed to measure whether your goals and communication are as clear as you believe them to be. Nothing cuts through the BS faster than the 'six-year-old' test.

It is exactly as it sounds: explain your idea or process to a child, preferably five, six or seven years old (if you don't 'own' one, get their parents' permission lest you look creepy). In doing so you will discover something powerful. In order to convey meaning, not just talk, you need to keep your words simple. A long, drawn-out explanation will bore them, so you need to make it interesting, you need to keep it simple and it needs to be complete.

TAKE SOMETHING OFF

Coco Chanel's impeccable taste also drew from the wisdom of simplicity and it is she who gave us a famous piece of fashion advice based on simplicity: 'Always take off the last thing you put on'.

This piece of wisdom is as pertinent to the way we communicate and do business as it is to fashion. Today we should always ask, 'What can we take off?' In other words, before you send that email, publish that report, share that vision or communicate that position, stop and ask what you can lose.

At this point it seems wise to mention that before you get up at your next board meeting and announce, 'Let's all take something off,' be sure to share the Chanel story first.

SIMPLIFY THE STEPS

The simpler you can make a process or transaction, the more likely others are to engage with it.

The adult 'toy' industry is benefiting enormously from the simplification of the buying process. Real-world storefronts are almost extinct, while online sales are booming. In fact, the industry is now worth $15 billion. There are two drivers at play here: one is the elimination of the embarrassment (Think Scared); the other is the simplification of buying, the online component (Think Stupid).

By simplifying the process and removing the visit to the store, we don't have to deal with our emotions or traffic or that someone else sees us entering at street level, let alone being lost and confused in a place we want to get out of as quickly as possible lest we bump into someone we know.

By Thinking Scared and Stupid, the adult toy industry is buzzing (apologies).

USE FEWER WORDS

In the digital age, everything has become abbreviated—our time, our interactions, our relationships and even our language. Words that originated in the world of texting have found their way into everyday usage: LOL, GTG and TGIF to name a few.

TED too has revolutionised speech lengths and arguably shortened attention spans. Where once a keynote speech may have lasted 45 minutes or an hour, today we see a trend towards 18 to 20 minutes. As speakers, this format forces us to choose our words and ideas wisely—to distil our thinking and be clear about the messages we want our audience to walk away with.

As globalisation continues to shape our world, we have even moved to communication with no words whatsoever. The visual is the one true global language, and an ability to share stories with only images is simple and powerful.

BASIC NEEDS ARE PRETTY BASIC

Bill Bernbach was a legend of the advertising industry back in the 1950s and 1960s. Many of his insights are as true today as they were then. Mr Bernbach was a great advocate of simple ideas and messages. He was also fascinated by the simple and unchanging nature of human beings, things that really don't change so much because they are human needs, not fashion. As young advertising executives decades later we were struck by how relevant his thoughts still were: 'A communicator must be concerned with the *unchanging* man, with ... his obsessive drive to survive, to be admired, to succeed, to love, to take care of his own ...'

Not much has changed and today Bill's wisdom stands true. At the end of the day we are simple creatures with simple emotional needs that do not fundamentally change, even while the world around us does.

Strive for simplicity for no other reason than this. Keep it simple by keeping what you are truly trying to achieve at the heart of what you do.

APPLYING 'MAKE IT SIMPLE'

When applying 'Make it simple', remember the following:

1 Remember that confusion paralyses us, so keep it simple.

2 Resist the urge to use complexity to convey sophistication.

3 If it is too hard, it really is too hard.

4 Learn to curate information, reputation and collaboration.

5 Apply Post-it Note discipline to your communications.

6 Take the 'six-year-old' test.

7 Remember that our basic needs are always pretty basic.

CHAPTER 11

Make it easy (lazy)

*I will always choose a lazy person to do a difficult job because
they will always find an easy way to do it.*

Bill Gates

As you travel around the world, you find that in addition to
extraordinary sculpture, evocative paintings, inspiring architecture
and an exquisite variety of performing arts, the world is also filled
with monuments to human laziness.

HUMAN BEINGS ARE NOTORIOUSLY LAZY

Anyone who has visited a major airport in the past decade will likely
have encountered the moving walkway. It is exactly as it sounds,
a long section of floor that moves you towards your destination at
a comfortable pace, removing the need for unnecessary walking or
other forms of self-propulsion.

Now, before the more energetic of you feel horribly impugned and
point out that you only use the travelator to increase the speed of your
gait and that you do in fact continue to utilise your bipedal appendages,
we'd like to draw your attention to the sign that always accompanies
these moving walkways. It always conveys an admonition for the

majority of us to keep to the right or left (depending on the part of the world you are in), on the off chance that one of you energetic types would like to pass by unhindered. In other words, while they clearly expect most of us to let the floor do the work for us, they don't want us to become human cholesterol and clog up our gloomily decorated arteries.

But this is not just a feature of the digital age. Back in the 1970s, as we all sat comfortably on our sofas watching television (still largely in black and white) we imagined a day when a device would sit in our hands, without a length of wire or other encumbrances, that might enable us to change the channel or adjust the volume using the fewest muscle groups possible.

However today, lazy, labour-saving devices are everywhere—we have microwave food, speed dating, online shopping, electronic mail … and so the list goes on.

LAZINESS IS THE MOTHER OF INVENTION

It is worth remembering that all advancement and all successful innovation delivered in the past few decades has been principally driven by one of two metrics: first, a reduction in the size of the product we use (although the 'my smartphone is bigger than yours' war is bucking the trend and returning us to good-old 'size matters' debates); and second, an increase in the ease of their use. For every modern convenience you enjoy—everything that makes life just that little bit better, more efficient or less fiddly—you can thank laziness.

This makes laziness a key component in leadership and innovation. Innovation is often conceived of as the creative process of invention, but as Oded Shenkar of The Ohio State University reveals in his research, 97.8 per cent of the value of an innovation goes to the imitator, which is not to say that innovation is an inherently lazy process, but merely that its success is not defined by creativity or invention. True innovation is actually a leadership skill, a capacity for category leadership, the ability to define the future course of an entire industry or market—something that may be achieved just as well by the lazy as the dedicated.

However, that is not how we like to think of laziness at a conscious or even a cultural level. Laziness is demonised to such an extent that it has changed our entire values system and even the language we employ to describe those values. Greet anyone in the modern world today and inquire as to their wellbeing and you're likely to get the automatic response, 'I'm busy … busy, busy, busy …' For all the time-saving devices that proliferate in our society, our society itself is apparently on the brink of an exhaustion that makes our farm-labouring, coal-mining ancestors look virtually idle by comparison.

Of course, this is largely a misunderstanding of the true busyness of our lives. Most of us are not ridiculously busy or even continuously occupied; we are in fact simply disorganised, or rather, poorly prioritised and easily distracted. And yet, busyness and overwork are now seen as badges of such social virtue that daring to take an annual holiday is something we almost apologise for.

We were invited to speak at a conference where the opening speakers appeared to be engaged in a competition to demonstrate who enjoyed the fewest hours of sleep.

'If you want to beat the competition, you need to be up at 6 am,' one proudly proclaimed. The next speaker insinuated 6 am was for losers and that only a 5 am start would get the deals done. '4 am!' the next suggested, not to be outdone by his predecessors. As you might expect, the audience, although interested in success, seemed less than enthused by the prospect of a 4 am start.

At this point, it may be worth pointing out that research published in *The Journal of Neuroscience* by researchers at the Center for Sleep and Circadian Neurobiology at the University of Pennsylvania, suggests that while early risers may be highly productive, sleep deprivation may in fact permanently and irreversibly kill brain cells (as opposed to the reversible kind of killing, presumably). This may suggest that the merits of being highly productive are somewhat offset by the stupidity of what is actually produced.

In a complete departure from this line of thinking, Tim Ferriss's *The 4-Hour Work Week* has been such a runaway success that it suggests two things: first, that our outward busyness may belie a secret longing for a little—or perhaps a lot—more 'me' time; and second, that perhaps busyness is not all it's cracked up to be.

In some respects, working hard is quite a lazy thing to do. 'How?', we hear you ask incredulously. It's simple. Putting your head down and labouring away with a production-line mentality requires much less active thinking and strategy than working in a thoughtful, proactive way. It's easy to be productive, but are you actually being productive in the right way and in the right activities?

Certainly, there are those of us who do have incredibly complicated lives where excellent parenting skills cohabit with running successful businesses, working as directors on boards, training the kids' sports teams and the like. Sometimes, these activities all happen within the one person in a single week. However, what is true for these successthletes, and for the rest of us, is that none of us has a second longer than anyone else during which to be busy.

What this suggests is that work–life prioritisation may be equally served by good judgement and the application of a little focused laziness. In other words, laziness may just help us use our time well.

HOW MIGHT LAZY BE EFFICIENT?

Kurt Gebhard Adolf Philipp Freiherr von Hammerstein-Equord was born to a noble family in Hinrichshagen, Mecklenburg-Strelitz, Germany, in 1878 and joined the German Army on 15 March 1898.

Between World War I and World War II, as chief of the Army High Command, Hammerstein-Equord oversaw the writing of the German manual on military unit command, known as Truppenführung, dated 17 October 1933.

Although the quote that you will find further down the page is occasionally attributed to his successor, field marshal Erich von Manstein, a man who himself regarded Hammerstein-Equord as, '...one of the cleverest people I ever met', it is largely believed to be the thinking of the former.

He is quoted as originating a special classification for his men based on how the intrinsic nature of their characters reflected on their performance:

'I divide my officers into four groups. There are clever, diligent, stupid, and lazy officers. Usually two characteristics are combined. Some are clever and diligent—their place is the General Staff. The next lot are stupid and lazy, they make up 90 per cent of every army and are suited to routine duties. Anyone who is both clever and lazy is qualified for the highest leadership duties, because he possesses the intellectual clarity and the composure necessary for difficult decisions. One must beware of anyone who is stupid and diligent—he must not be entrusted with any responsibility because he will always cause only mischief'.

It's worth remembering that while both men ended up on the wrong side of history post–World War II, Hammerstein-Equord's capacity to read character was such that he violently opposed the Nazis and Hitler, a decision that cost him his post and rank before World War II began, but ultimately proved his capacity to read people accurately.

The theory is as relevant today as it was in the 1930s. If we're completely honest about it, most employees are not career warriors driven to achieve ever-increasing business goals and push their personal performance to new heights. For many, if not most, of us a job is just a job; that is, simply a way of providing for our material needs and those of our family.

This is not to say that we don't want to do a good job, nor that we are not capable. It's simply that human beings, for the most part, are not especially willing to make an extraordinary effort to achieve these goals. As much as we may call this kind of thinking lazy, disrespectful or even ungrateful, it is what is. What's more, the desire for an easier, more efficient solution is perhaps something to be encouraged.

And yet, rather than factoring this understanding into our systems and approaches to behavioural strategy, we spend our lives berating teenagers for not making their beds, and our staff for taking personal calls or indulging in a little social media sharing. We chide ourselves for our lack of motivation, for not being as wealthy as we should be, for not training this morning, for not standing up for ourselves or even for a few moments of day dreaming on a busy day.

It is our considered opinion that this has the potential to be a spectacular error in judgement.

As we've asserted throughout this book, changing people's behaviour is extremely difficult, and perhaps rather than criticising what seems to be a rather universal characteristic, we should instead design the systems we work within in accordance with our natures. In other words, how could we make the work we strive to do, congruent and achievable with an appropriate amount of ease?

We're not talking about creating a culture of slothful layabouts who feel so uninspired they make Homer Simpson look like Employee of the Month. We're suggesting that the systems we build should make it easy to get things done and get them done correctly. Rather than relying on talent and performance alone, we should engineer systems so that they work even on days when our engagement and performance is not what it could be.

This may seem rather defeatist. As revealed in Gallup's 2013 workplace-engagement study (which we discussed in chapter 4), 20 per cent of your workforce is white-anting the labour of the other 80 per cent (although Gallup's statistics also suggest that possibly only half of that number actually care).

This finding means that it is critical that we design processes and cultures, and the structure of the work we do with lazy and stupid in mind. This must happen so that the disengaged 20 to 50 per cent of the workforce can actually deliver results such that the other 50 per cent of our engaged workers are free to lift their performance in areas they currently don't have time for (principally because they're carrying a disproportionate percentage of the load). We will talk more about this in a moment.

EASE RAISES CONFIDENCE AND COMPETENCE

We're not suggesting that everything in life should be easy. In fact, striving is an important factor when it comes to motivating people. Human resources studies reveal time and time again that we feel most motivated when we are engaged in a pursuit that stretches us. However, and this is an important caveat, this is only when the stretch feels within our capabilities.

What this means is that ease may be best defined as 'a reasonable expectation combined with sufficient resourcing'.

Despite the overwhelming availability of this kind of research, corporate culture is far from populated by reasonable expectation or sufficient resourcing. It is mostly defined by empty platitudes such as, 'Give 110 per cent' or 'If you don't come in on Saturday, don't bother coming in on Sunday!' In other words, do more with less ... or else.

Our schools also seem to have adopted this, 'I'll sleep when I'm dead' attitude, which coincidentally seems to align with the phenomenon of student burnout. So it is, also, with our personal goals. Our culture tells us that if we're not rich, famous, sexual Olympians with abdominals you could bounce a coin off and a captivating personality we are somehow social losers. In response, we internalise these expectations and punish ourselves mentally and physically even when our goal was actually to do something mentally and physically nice for ourselves.

Life will not always be without its struggles, but in addressing these struggles, we increase our chances of success by employing strategies that make the struggle seem less so.

A colleague of ours, Dr Adam Fraser, in his book *The Third Space* reveals that one of the principal ingredients for lifting your performance in any sphere of your life is not what you do in the moments of activity, but what you choose to do in the moments in-between, in what he calls 'the third space'. This indicates that we intuitively understand that when we engage in highly demanding activities, none of us is capable of being permanently 'on' and it is only in allowing moments of ease and in reducing the strain and the demand of the activities we perform that we can sustain high performance over a prolonged period.

And yet this idea of 'go hard or go home' persists, while the quest for ease is somehow seen as belonging to an inferior mindset. Today, virtually no-one would suggest that the haulage of large stone blocks should employ the technology of the ancient Egyptians (with long lines of people pulling on ropes tied to a single block as it rumbles over wooden cylinders cut from nearby trees). That would be ludicrous. Any strategy that didn't involve the use of a crane and a large semi-trailer powered by an internal combustion engine would be seen as foolhardy and even indicative of diminished faculties.

As ridiculous as this example seems, we employ precisely this kind of judgement virtually every day when we push our people to work hard in systems that are outdated and no longer support their capacity or competency—and actually shun any change of process 'just to make things easier'!

So how can we make our daily grind less grinding? What does it take to make work easier, more efficient and more enjoyable? And how can we turn our inherent laziness into an asset that works incredibly hard, even when we don't?

Reduce the friction points

This point seems almost ridiculously obvious, but virtually every organisation has within it processes that actually make getting what needs to be done, more difficult. Departments with interconnecting roles run software programs that don't speak to each other, sales processes actually make it harder for customers to pay organisations, customer support is under-resourced, staff training sits at the bottom of to-do lists, legal departments say 'no' so often that their co-workers begin referring to them as the 'Department of no' and leaders set direct reporting metrics and measures that contradict each other.

However, reducing these friction points not only increases our efficiency and productivity, it also enables these increases to be more easily maintained.

The fast-food drive-through window is a perfect example of this. (Before you put your soap box up on top of your high horse and complain about the evils of fast food, we'd just like to point out that getting out of your car in no way improves the food's quality.)

Certainly, the goal of fast food is implicit in the title. The invention of the drive-through not only enables an already lazy process of not preparing your own food to be even easier, it also enables the business to drive greater numbers of customers through their service area while reducing face-to-face customer contact and the requirement to invest in more parking spots.

Make it look easy or intuitive

The success of Apple—the computer company, not the fruit—is due in no small part to the driving ethos behind every product it has brought to the marketplace. This ethos was already evident in Apple's marketing in the 1970s: 'a computer for the rest of us'.

At a time when the world of computers was reserved for those who could read code and understand the secret language required, Apple launched a PC with a visual interface. It had a Trash icon into which you deposited your 'trash', and folders you could put your files into, all by dragging a pointer around the screen and clicking on a mouse. It was a revolution that democratised access to technology.

This ideology has driven every success Apple has brought to the marketplace: the wheel on the iPod that made accessing files a thumb-based activity; the swiping and pinching actions on the iPad; even Siri, which reduces the friction in digital interaction by enabling you to ask for what you want verbally.

Every great success from this extraordinary organisation is not based on their technological brilliance, nor is it because they market on price point. It is driven by their capacity to make what they do look easy, accessible and intuitive.

Equalise the effort

Every time you add a new system or process within your organisation, even if you believe it makes your staff's work easier, you have actually made their lives more difficult. In other words, adding additional layers without removing existing ones is not a simplification, it's simply another chore for the day.

We worked with a European-based multinational organisation that had brought us in to help them build a culture of more open collaboration and innovation. To kick off this new initiative, they had organised for all of their senior managers to come together in one city to announce the new initiative (and also to announce some other changes we were not privy to).

These 'other changes' became apparent as soon as the operations manager stepped up to the microphone and announced, '... we've also decided to give you some additional KPIs ... but you'll like these ones. They'll help you do your jobs better ...'.

Hmmmm! Quite an opening! Not only had our new initiative been prefaced with the implication that the top brass believed their staff were delivering below par, they would also be asked to implement yet another metric to be measured against and have another task to add to their daily to-do lists. Hardly the motivational introduction we'd hoped for.

It's not that you shouldn't introduce new processes, measures or projects to people's to-do lists, but rather that when you do, you would be well advised to equalise the effort. In other words, think of all new activities in terms of trade-offs. Ideally, a new process should replace two existing processes, or at the very least, the number of steps involved in getting the job done well shouldn't increase. By equalising, or in fact reducing, the number of steps involved, you not only increase the chances of success, you increase your influence within your organisation.

Limit the number of steps (and intermediaries)

When Dan wanted to buy himself a new motorcycle, he spent a huge amount of time researching the exact bike he wanted and developed a relationship with the salesperson at the local Harley Davidson store. She was great. She knew her motorcycles, accommodated every pernickety enquiry he made with the patience of Job and helped him design the perfect bike. Dan was thrilled and built an enormous amount of trust with this salesperson as a result of the process.

Then, at the most critical point of the sales process—what we call the 'break point' of the sale; that is, the moment when contracts would be signed and money would change hands—she led him into the office of someone Dan had never met before and left while this stranger informed Dan he would be taking his money. Trust immediately left the room and Dan was left with a feeling of post-purchase dissonance, only this was happening even before he'd even handed over the money.

Increasing the number of steps to make the sale—increasing the number of intermediaries or hands that the prospect has to pass through—costs more sales conversions than just about any other behaviour in the sales process.

What you are essentially doing is increasing the number of break points in the process. Considering that the above example added a second break point to what is the *critical* break point of a sale—the signing of contracts and exchanging of funds—this process has the potential to be sales suicide.

What this really represented was not a drive for efficiency, but a lack of empowerment for a critical member of the sales team. In other words, the process didn't allow for the salesperson with whom the relationship had been built to perform at her best and complete the sale.

Be hard on delivery but flexible on process

Often, we can micromanage those we lead to such a degree that not only do we fail to inspire autonomous performance, we in fact reduce the effectiveness of our team and ourselves entirely.

One of the most valuable ways we can learn to use the human tendency for laziness as an asset is to allow it greater freedom. Initially this may seem like a folly that will inevitably go horribly wrong. But an interesting thing happens when you give someone greater responsibility for their own behaviour (with an agreed series of deliverables and deadlines of course): they panic (a little). In other words, responsibility brings with it its own sense of fear. And that can be highly motivating.

The truth is, while most people protest that they want more responsibility, when they actually receive it, it tends to look rather more like pressure.

One of the most unexpected leadership stories of autonomy with accountability comes from David Lee Roth, the lead singer of the band Van Halen.

The story has it that while the band was touring, Lee Roth had a proviso written into the band's rider (the part of the contract that is signed with the promoter). This proviso instructed the production crew that back stage at every concert there had to be a huge bowl of M&Ms with all of the brown M&Ms removed. On the surface of it, this seems like an extremely rock star, prima donna thing to do. However, a Van Halen show has a lot of moving parts, pyrotechnics, lighting and sound connections. In other words, there are a lot of opportunities for failure. Clearly Mr Lee Roth didn't have time to personally check that his team had done all of their work meticulously, but then he didn't have to. A single brown M&M was all he needed to suggest he should get his people to recheck all of their connections.

By being hard on results and flexible on process, we actually enable people to deliver what we need in a way that also satisfies their needs.

APPLYING 'MAKE IT EASY (LAZY)'

When applying 'Make it easy (lazy)', remember the following:

1 Reduce the friction in the process by making it more intuitive.

2 Demonstrate how simplifying streamlines difficult processes.

3 Equalise the effort by swapping out activities rather than simply adding to the list of required to-dos.

4 Communicate how simplifying processes makes your day less of a headache by making things look easy.

5 Limit the number of steps and hands the process must go through as every increment will naturally become a resistance point.

6 Be hard on results and flexible on process. The more autonomy you allow and the greater the clarity around the key deliverables, the greater the responsibility that will be taken.

CHAPTER 12

Make it hard not to

Scuttle the ships.

Hernán Cortés

For most of the modern era of behavioural research and strategy, activities such as advertising, staff training, public-service announcements and information-based campaigning have relied almost exclusively on appealing to our logical or emotional intelligence in order to achieve the desired change. This is as true of sales scripts as it is of habit rehabilitation programs, public awareness campaigns and the communication of occupational health and safety standards. In other words, in an effort to change behaviour, the tools of choice have principally been influence and persuasion.

CHANGING OPINIONS VERSUS CHANGING BEHAVIOUR

However, more recently there has been an increasing push to change behaviour by changing behaviour (which sounds exceedingly obvious when you say it out loud but it really is quite new in its popularity). However, this process is a bit less intuitive, or indeed culturally favoured, than you may at first expect. This is partially because our previous experiences of such strategies have been with systems that were less than democratic, and have even involved force, violence and otherwise unethical coercion.

This rather challenging history of 'change-driven change' aside, whenever we do try to correct a habit, shift a business process or even change the behaviour of large parts of the community for their own benefit, it's worth remembering that simply offering information, or even a persuasive argument, is seldom enough to get the job done.

This is due, in no small part, to the fact that we very rarely operate out of a logical or even emotional consciousness. Most of our activity is in fact unconscious. This, as it turns out, is rather a good thing as it streamlines our lives and makes day-to-day activities less of a chore. Can you imagine how complicated the process of simply getting out the door each morning would be if we had to analyse and strategise whenever a decision had to be made?

Thankfully, as we grow up and learn our way in the world, many of our decisions in life become relegated to the 'I've got that sorted' pile and eventually fall into our subconscious as almost instinctive responses. What this means, however, is that we rarely take the time to reflect or audit whether these decisions—often made in years gone by—are still relevant, based in reality or even particularly productive. In fact, such questions come to be immensely annoying and are firmly put in their place whenever we are forced to go over old ground.

What's more, questions around the efficacy of our behaviour internally may be one thing, but the idea that anyone else might question our behaviour and have the temerity to suggest that there may be a better way is, frankly, unbearable.

All of this means that logical and emotional appeals often fall on deaf ears and hardened hearts and we become so resistant to change that we begin to think of this resistance as a virtue. Certainly, to suggest that a friend has 'changed' or that they are 'not who they used to be' is rarely meant as a compliment.

WE WILL RESIST CHANGE IF WE CAN

People often say extraordinary things, such as, 'Change is as good as a holiday,' then we all nod as if some great truth has been revealed that we were all aware of but had hitherto not put into words. Of course, although it is a pithy little maxim and we may indeed find that change can be incredibly refreshing, it is however complete nonsense! Just try putting change in a staff member's employment contract in place of their annual leave entitlement and you'll pretty quickly see just how valuable change actually is.

Human history, rather than being a story of how change has been embraced and cherished, is peppered with upheaval, war, grudges that have lasted centuries and violent uprisings, all in the name of maintaining the status quo. What's more, having the truth, or even scientific fact, on your side is no guarantee of success. It took roughly one thousand years and the execution of quite a number of so-called heretics before there was an acceptance of a heliocentric solar system and the round earth theory — and these can be proved with equipment as crude as a watch, a stick and a ruler capable of measuring the length of a shadow.

Even in our modern age, where change has reached a logarithmic pace, we still strain against change wherever it confronts us. And confront us it does!

Every time a social network such as Facebook changes their design or visual interface in even the slightest way, blogs, protests and social movements spring up in opposition almost overnight. When Coca-Cola tried to reinvigorate its business by introducing a reformulated 'New Coke' it almost destroyed one of the most iconic brands on earth. And when Burger King decided to test its customer's loyalty by removing its 'Whopper' sandwich from the menu for just one day in one store in the United States, its customers were so outraged, they demanded to see the manager, complained to the waiting media that this was a travesty and suggested that if Burger King doesn't have the Whopper it may as well change its name to Burger Queen!

The implicit sexism of this remark aside, this 'Whopper freakout' demonstrates the irrational anger, indignation and resistance even the most inconsequential of changes can arouse in the human population.

And so it is with all change. We resist it because we fear it. We resist it because it forces us to evaluate the existing pre-fabricated decisions we use to navigate and streamline the complexity of life. And crucially, we resist change because we quite enjoy the status quo. It's comfortable, it's familiar and let's be honest, it enables us to lazily cruise through life with a minimum of effort.

What this means for those of us who lead—those who wish to usher in change and shift long-held perceptions or truly have an influence in our communities—is that we need a more strategic approach than simply talking about the change we want, even when it's emotionally intelligent talk.

To simply know is not enough. To believe is not enough. To want to is not enough. You must also drive change at a behavioural level, be willing to 'scuttle the ships', as Hernán Cortés counselled his men as they ruthlessly pursued Montezuma's gold. His reasoning was simple: when the only alternative is death ... you find a way to make it work!

THE RISE OF BEHAVIOURAL ECONOMICS

The development of the behavioural economics school of thought tends to align with this kind of thinking. It assumes that many of the mistakes we make are not made at a conscious or rational level, but are systemic and so we need a more systematic approach in order to change.

Dan Ariely, in his book *Predictably Irrational: The Hidden Forces that Shape Our Decisions* notes that, 'Standard economics assumes that we are rational ... But ... we are far less rational in our decision making ... Our irrational behaviours are neither random nor senseless—they are systematic and predictable. We all make the same types of mistakes over and over, because of the basic wiring of our brains'.

What behavioural economics seeks to achieve, without trying to be disrespectful, is to rebrand and distinguish itself from other branches of psychology and create some distance from behavioural strategists, who prefer the more cognitive and emotional approach, and its own preference for a more physical or active approach to change.

On one side you have a group that essentially asserts that belief drives behaviour while the other insists that this is reading the equation backwards. In practice, however, as is the case with all properly balanced equations, the truth always runs both ways. For the purposes of this chapter, it is worth spending some time considering the behavioural economics ethos more fully as this is often the part of behavioural change that is most overlooked and underutilised.

It's useful to think of this distinction as roughly equivalent to the distinctions pertaining to people's learning styles. It's suggested that some people are visual learners and some are auditory. Others need to have an empathic feel for the instruction, while another group prefers kinaesthetic learning, or learning by doing. Of course, this too is an oversimplification and it would be unwise to suggest that an auditory learner cannot learn visually or is unable to read without sub-vocalising. Having said this, we do naturally have a bias to particular styles of learning and these approximately correlate with different theories of behavioural change.

In the above comparison, behavioural economists would roughly assume a similar position to kinaesthetic learners. In other words, they may argue that as we learn by doing, we in fact change by doing change as opposed to simply understanding by visual demonstration or by receiving aural instructions.

What behavioural economics offers us is a more complete picture and toolkit with which to assess and access change in the real world. We would argue that while it does not replace or devalue the persuasive arts, it does add to our suite of strategies for managing and in fact driving change.

PLACE BARRIERS IN THE PATH OF UNWANTED BEHAVIOUR

Although placing barriers may seem like an incredibly logical strategy for driving change, it is one that we fear is rather too rarely used. This is partly because it seems like something we would employ to keep a child safe, such as kitchen cupboard locks and gates at the top of a stairwell, rather than something we would use for our own behaviour or in a corporate environment.

However, it is also another of the casualties of the positivism movement, where any instruction that may have a negative connotation is considered an inferior mode of motivation.

This incessant need to be 'positive' has become so pervasive that it has rendered even simple pieces of communication ridiculously complicated.

Some time ago we were engaged by a railroad for a particular region to help them develop a safety program for their commuters. It turns out that far too many of them were dying as a result of misadventure on the tracks. This was due to a variety of reasons including suicide, vandalism by graffiti 'artists' and pure human laziness because people decided a shortcut was worth the risk.

While this may seem a simple enough issue to understand, the caveat they made for how we might approach this problem was that the solution had to be overwhelmingly positive. There was to be no use of negative language (such as the words 'no' or 'don't'), it couldn't imply negative consequence (such as injury, death, stupidity or the dismay of one's loved ones) and it could not use 'coercive' or restrictive behavioural strategies (such as fences or limiting access) to achieve the desired results.

When Dan inquired whether a message such as, 'Stay off the rails and keep your life on track' was what they were looking for, instead of receiving the desired mild rebuke for the implied sarcasm, they instead indicated that they rather liked the ending but the first bit was a bit negative.

Suffice to say, it was not really the kind of client relationship our organisation invests in as clearly they were more interested in ensuring the increasing number of corpses on their tracks died with a sense of positive enthusiasm than being negatively realistic and perhaps saving a few lives.

However, some public entities have embraced a fuller behavioural strategy for driving change. In recent decades, in an effort to develop a more inclusive and responsible approach to our use of resources and the disposal of the waste and refuse they produce, local governments have actively encouraged their constituents to sort through their rubbish and actively participate in the recycling process.

Initially, this began with organising recycling collections, where specially commissioned trucks roamed city and suburban streets collecting recyclable materials that were left on the footpath in a container that was itself recyclable, such as a cardboard box. It was an encouraging beginning to be sure, but as anyone who lives in a high precipitation area will have immediately identified, not the most practical solution, nor one that leaves the footpath looking like it belongs in a community that has a responsible view towards its trash.

The immediate solution was obvious. Another rubbish bin, or recycling bin, was called for. Of course, this presented another opportunity to not simply inform citizens of the need for recycling, but to influence their behaviour in a rather more tangible way.

Today, as you travel around the majority of the developed world, you will notice that virtually no home, office or shopping mall for that matter, will offer you just one receptacle for your trash, waste paper or assorted genres of rubbish. Most homes now have a container designated for green waste (such as lawn clippings); one for recycling of glass, plastics and paper waste; and of course another for general rubbish that doesn't meet the criteria of the other two grades of trash.

Moreover, in a move designed not just to inspire recycling but also to reduce the amount of general waste each household and business produces, the rubbish bin, or more often the plastic 'wheelie bin' that many local councils designate for general waste is significantly smaller than the other two, often 50 per cent smaller (even when both of the bins are collected with the same frequency). Not only are you encouraged to sort through your rubbish and recycle more, you are subtly coerced into adopting behaviour that limits the amount of waste that simply goes to landfill (or else you are forced to resort to late night stealth tactics as you try to sneak your excess rubbish into the neighbour's wheelie bin as quietly as is humanly possible).

LIMIT THE AVAILABLE OPTIONS

This strategy is akin to placing barriers in the way of a behaviour you want to change, but it is slightly more nuanced and systems based.

Limiting choices or options is a significant strategy in changing people's behaviour in any sphere, partly because it steers us towards a preferred option, but more importantly, because it works to reduce indecisiveness and procrastination.

One of the ironies of human behaviour is that increased levels of choice typically lead to increased indecisiveness. On one level, this is a completely rational assumption. If there is only once choice on the table, the decision is automatic, or at least very nearly automatic.

Often, this limitation of choice isn't simply a matter of limiting the number of options available. It may also inform how a system, product or behaviour is designed.

In other words, limitation of choice may be something as simple as making the usual or preferred choices bigger or more obvious. This is why, for example, the emergency stop button at a petrol station is quite deliberately hard to miss. They limit your options by making the one they want you to take stand out.

FRUSTRATE PREVIOUS BEHAVIOUR

One of the best examples of actively trying to frustrate existing behaviour while trying to implement the preferred behaviour is the development of transit lanes—lanes exclusively available to public modes of transport such as buses and taxis, and hired private cars such as limousines — on major highways.

In addition to these transit lanes are carpooling lanes, which offer cars with more than one passenger the opportunity to drive down a less congested part of the road.

Both of these strategies have been implemented in an effort to reduce traffic congestion on major roads, which will ultimately make driving on these roads more pleasurable and sustainable. However, initially, these measures will in fact often reduce the number of lanes available to privately driven cars and, in doing so, will actually create greater congestion and delays for drivers in the short term. While this seems counter intuitive, the reasoning is actually quite sound.

As the lanes designated for public transport, such as buses, and carpoolers are no longer available for lone private drivers, the preferred behaviour — public transport and shared commuting — flows more freely. This behaviour also acts to frustrate lone drivers, often to the point where they reluctantly seek alternatives such as carpooling or utilising the public options provided.

If you think this sounds incredibly manipulative, annoying and frustrating, you're right. It is. That's precisely the point.

And yet, this frustration may not always be permanent, and in fact as new behaviours are adopted and old ones left behind this frustration often gives way to acceptance, engagement and ultimately social endorsement.

Think about the war against big tobacco that most governments around the developed world are now engaged in. What started as public-health information campaigns, led to emotionally provocative and quite grotesque scare campaigns. These were later augmented with changes made to physical behaviour such as smoking bans in hospitals, workplaces, restaurants and bars. It's now become virtually impossible to smoke within three metres of the doorway of a public building in some countries.

What used to be a social habit is now something you can only enjoy 'in your own home, under a blanket with the lights out' to quote Denis Leary. And even then, that's only if you don't have a vulnerable child in the house.

The key learning here is that while creating barriers to previous undesired behaviours or simply making them more annoying may result in some initial discomfort and pushback, it can in fact drive sustainable change in the long term. This is particularly the case when it is paired with an alternative behaviour that is exceptionally convenient.

MAKE THE PREFERRED BEHAVIOUR MORE AVAILABLE

Of course, the converse to putting barriers between people and the undesired behaviour and thereby limiting their choices is to make the preferred behaviour more available and more desirable.

This is the preferred strategy of the banking system, which has changed the way it serves its customers by using machines rather than people. It is part of an effort to reduce face-to-face contact and therefore labour costs (and let's not kid ourselves, those machines can be a lot more efficient than your typical bank teller). Initially, the banks cut a hole in the walls of their buildings, replaced the bricks and mortar with a computer and filled it with cash and, as comedian Jack Dee observed, more than a little attitude in some cases: 'Funds not available ... and I think you know why ...'

These cash-dispensing machines are now available everywhere. Moreover, the local supermarket is now licensed to provide the same cash withdrawal service that was once the exclusive domain of the banking sector and the uptake of computer chipped credit and debit card technology is well on the way to removing the need for cash at all.

In most first-world countries outside the United States, even the use of cheques has virtually disappeared as electronic funds transfers—once the sole domain of bank staff with a suitable level of seniority—are now the preferred method of receiving wages and salaries, paying bills, contributing to a collective pool for a birthday gift and even paying tolls on private highways. The last no longer even asks for your credit card details. A small transmitter in your car linked to your account simply 'beeps' as you pass by the collection point.

In all of this, the preferred behaviour has been made more available and simpler, and it has reduced the amount of work involved to make the transaction happen.

As the availability of the alternative service rises, so does its uptake. Distribution has long been a strategy of success for corporations such as Coca-Cola, whose mantra is to be 'within an arm's length of desire'. And so it is with all behavioural change: our capacity to utilise environmental factors such as distribution, focused restriction and strategic frustration, as well as providing the opportunity for social endorsement, is critical to a fuller behavioural change strategy.

What this really equates to is increasing the proximity of the preferred behaviour. Proximity offers simplicity and ease while reducing effort. In doing so, it reduces the need for discipline and extrinsic motivation.

CONTROL THE ENVIRONMENT

A better description than behavioural economics for the psychology of change may be environmental economics, although this tends to connote images of hippies chained to trees trying to protect old growth forests. The ambiguity of the word 'environment' aside, it still represents a more descriptive and satisfactory title for explaining what the entire process of change requires. Changes at a logical and emotional level require environmental changes in how beliefs are asserted, shared and transmitted and changes at a behavioural and social level necessitate the designing of environments and systems in which people can operate in new ways with limited push back.

This need for an environmental approach to change is something we faced while working with a foundation that helped fund research into diabetes. Given that type 2 diabetes is a metabolic disorder whose incidence and treatment are fundamentally linked to diet and physical activity, we were brought in to help develop strategies for creating positive change in these two areas. This, incidentally, is the change that has baffled the majority of the medical, psychological and fitness community for more than a century—so a nice and easy challenge then!

On the plus side, we had just been delivered some amazing scientific research into the dietary and exercise practices that would best drive this outcome in a sustainable and enjoyable way, unlike most of the diets in popular circulation today. However, as you may suspect, given the scale of the problem in our society, this wasn't going to be sufficient to drive the change we wanted. Neither was simply delivering a new diet discovery likely to engender a response greater than an exasperated sigh.

One of the issues we faced was that this is such a community-wide epidemic that an environmental approach was decidedly difficult to test and implement from a logistics point of view, even with a hefty budget (which we didn't have).

The plan we ended up presenting, therefore, enabled us to make the budget work at an environmental level. We decided to focus on precincts rather than entire communities and to prototype through corporate partnerships and then duplicate and share our successes. What this meant at a practical level was that we would be able to control discrete environments such as corporate parks—discrete communities where large corporations base their operations.

These corporate parks are often outside central city locations and are purpose built as precincts where people work, but do not live. As a result, they are often underserved in terms of human infrastructure and services. What they do allow for, however, is control.

Our strategy was to involve, educate and incentivise the staff at these organisations (covering off the cognitive and emotional side), as well as changing the menu offered in canteens, cafeterias and convenience stores operating on the property with enjoyable and clearly coded options (which helped support change at a behavioural level). We would also challenge them to redesign the structure of the workday so that exercise and recreation time was actively supported by the corporations involved in the interest of maintaining and improving the health of their staff.

The quid pro quo for the corporations was healthier, more engaged, more energetic staff and the opportunity to create a spirit of community and sociability based on good health within these often 'soulless' corporate parks.

While this is still a prototype model of how large-scale behavioural change could be applied, it serves to illustrate how effective change should be modelled on more than just changing opinions or simply being coercive with behaviour.

A more holistic approach—where the systems and processes work with human nature and enable change to come naturally, sustainably and, just as importantly, with a level of enjoyment and social reward—makes change voluntary, sticky and enthusiastic.

APPLYING 'MAKE IT HARD NOT TO'

When applying 'Make it hard not to', remember the following:

1 Create obstructions between yourself and the behaviour you're trying to remove or reduce.

2 Limit the options and choices available. In other words, don't let procrastination get in the way of change.

3 Make the previous or unwanted behaviour more frustrating and annoying to exercise.

4 Tilt the odds in your favour by increasing the availability of the preferred behaviour.

5 Control the environment in which the behaviour takes place in such a way that the desired behaviour is likely to follow.

SELFISH, SCARED AND STUPID IN THE REAL WORLD

If you've made it to this point of the book, well done! Statistics gathered by *The Huffington Post* suggest that, sadly, at least one quarter of those who are lucky and privileged enough to be literate haven't in fact read a single book in the past year. Worse, many of us will fail to ever read a book again after graduating college. Of those rare few seekers of knowledge who do bother to pick up a book, another disturbingly large number can't be bothered reading all the way through.

So, assuming you haven't just skipped to the conclusion to see how it ends, well done and thank you.

It has always been our goal in writing this book that we might pass on some of what we have learned in a combined half century of studying the intricacies of human nature in a format that enables each of our readers to apply this information in a way that is impactful and relevant to them. As to whether we have succeeded, we will leave that to your judgement.

By now, you will have hopefully realised that this book is fundamentally a treatise on how we can all engage our intrinsic natures rather than fighting them—that we may structure our lives, our businesses, our educations and our communities accordingly, and use this understanding of what truly drives our behaviour to pursue our goals more effectively and efficiently.

Too often, we limit our true potential by trying to force fit ourselves, and those around us, into methodologies and processes that are so at odds with the core motivations developed throughout our evolution on this planet that we fail quite unnecessarily. We deny our natures, our uniqueness and our worth.

Our wish for you is that you maximise your chances of success by working with the nature of human behaviour, not based on false claims or well-meaning fantasies.

The three principles that sit at the root of our internal motivation outlined in this book are not meant to be a quick fix of simple steps to follow, but rather they work like three interconnected tumblers of a combination lock that, when used correctly, will unlock human potential.

As you can see in figure 1, each tumbler is to be turned and adjusted until it clicks into position, enabling the right balance of each motivation to drive both the change desired and the individuals required.

Figure 1: the 'selfish, scared and stupid' combination lock

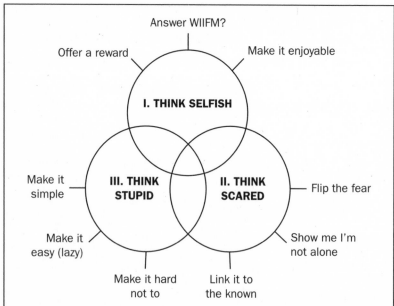

It's useful to think of this diagram as a combination lock rather than strictly as a Venn diagram. The goal is to adjust the balance of each lock sequentially to dial up your influence. Anchor it in self-interest; rebalance the fear from action to inaction; then reduce the friction in this action by making it simple, easy or hard not to.

The goal is to assess your individual situation and determine which facet needs to be dialled up or retuned.

FOR SELFISH, SCARED AND STUPID ENTREPRENEURS

For most small businesses, the most valuable assets in the organisation walk out the door every day at 5 pm. The value of the business, therefore, does not lie in the business itself, but is largely left to the success of hiring policies — or to luck.

The greatest step-change a small business can make is when the value of the intellectual property of the business — the proprietary processes, systems, brand guidelines and 'nowhere else experiences' — is independent of those who choose to work in its employ.

This is what enables a business to raise its worth, increase its resale value, franchise, scale, acquire and integrate. To do this well, our systems must be bulletproof, duplicable and, hence, selfish, scared and stupid.

FOR SELFISH, SCARED AND STUPID LEADERS

It has become cliché to assert that there is a difference between leaders and managers; what is rare, though, is clarity about what informs this distinction. Perhaps a helpful definition is simply that managers are appointed, whereas leaders ... well ... lead. One therefore gains authority from position; the other gathers followers.

In other words, what makes a great leader is not that they tell you what to do but that they help you realise what you could be. In doing so, they build a culture of the willing, the voluntary and the enthusiastic.

Leaders build environments and belief systems that inform our 'who, what and why', whereas managers inform the 'how'. A selfish, scared and stupid leader brings a measure of both—that is, an ability to demonstrate how their vision aligns with our goals, to give us the courage we need and to set a simple path for us to follow. They also engineer an environment that enables us to be motivated, supported, efficient and competent.

FOR SELFISH, SCARED AND STUPID TEAMS

What is it that makes a team world-class?

Is it simply having the best players on the field? Unlikely. You almost always have only the best you could afford given your budget of time and money to find and attract them.

Is it having the most resourced and highly trained? Perhaps not, given the frequency with which a boot-strapping start-up knocks off a hitherto market leader.

In fact, what makes a world-class team is a combination of things:

- enabling them to unlock their own personal genius and bring the greatest of their assets to the table
- creating an environment where they can realistically stretch themselves
- building systems that enable them to work quickly and confidently and to deliver results easily.

A great team, therefore, is as much defined by the competence of the coaching practices as it is by star players.

FOR SELFISH, SCARED AND STUPID BEHAVIOURAL CHANGE

It is always assumed that change is intrinsically hard. A more accurate sentiment could be to say that change is hard because of the resistance it encounters.

Making change not just possible, but adaptable, shareable and sustainable will be the skillset that defines success in the future. Change is on the increase and our tradition of barking new directions at our staff, ourselves and those we wish to influence will no longer cut it.

The change that will matter is that which is willing, voluntary, enthusiastic and lasting.

FOR SELFISH, SCARED AND STUPID SALES

The sale is virtually never in the product, it is always in the prospect.

The less you talk about yourself, your product, its features and its benefits and instead anchor your sell in your customer's identity — their self-interest — understand their fears and shift them from inaction to action while removing unnecessary friction and complication, the more charismatic, influential and persuasive you become.

FOR YOUR SELFISH, SCARED AND STUPID SELF

There is no way around it. You are selfish. You are scared. And you, like all of us, are (how shall we put this?) stupid! In other words, you are exquisitely human and have within you the extraordinary capacities that enabled our species to not only survive, but to thrive.

Rather than partitioning yourself into things you like and dislike, and instead of beating yourself up, endlessly criticising your foibles and disowning the 'shameful' parts of yourself, embrace it all. Embrace your nature, utilise your uniqueness and access the power of intrinsic motivation.

WE ARE ALL SELFISH, SCARED AND STUPID ... THANK GOODNESS

This is not a book that is designed to be negative or to question our infinite capacities as human beings, but rather a plea that we may develop an appreciation for the true natures that we have for too long dishonoured, denigrated and undervalued.

When we work with our human nature rather than trying to contort ourselves to fit into unworkable systems, we are more effective, efficient and enthusiastic.

And that is anything but selfish, scared and stupid.

THE IMPOSSIBLE INSTITUTE™

The Impossible Institute™ was founded to make what's not … possible!

HUMAN BEHAVIOUR AND BELIEF SYSTEMS

We exist to drive organisational and cultural change, helping build environments that lift performance and engagement.

In a world that is increasingly defined by our ability to adapt, innovate and engage, we advise sales departments and management on what truly drives their customers and staff to build highly functioning teams with Collaborative Intelligence™; apply discipline to creativity, removing the randomness and luck from Innovation and Strategy; and advise the C-Suite and boards on how to Lead with the Power of a Purposeful Identity.

Our curricula develop the people and processes within organisations, schools and social movements so that they have a lasting, mission-aligned capacity to generate multiple *answers*, autonomously.

We use a 'teach a man to fish' model because our research has told us that that's what works. Not only does this process generate more effective and measurable results, increased internal capabilities are also more profitable. They create greater team buy-in as well as external engagement and ultimately create a more valuable and enthusiastic workforce for our clients and their customers.

The four pillars of the institute are Speaking, Training, Strategy and Research. We run programs for corporations, small business and schools covering:

- Creative Leadership
- Creative Cultures
- Creative Insights
- Creative Selling
- Creative Learning

For more information, visit:

- www.theimpossibleinstitute.com
- @ImpossibleInst
- facebook.com/theimpossibleinstitute

INDEX

Learn more with practical advice from our experts

The Great Fragmentation
Steve Sammartino

The Game Changer
Dr Jason Fox

Winning the War for Talent
Mandy Johnson

It Starts With Passion
Keith Abraham

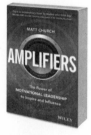

Amplifiers
Matt Church

Understanding Y
Charlie Caruso

Above the Line
Michael Henderson

Digilogue
Anders Sörman-Nilsson

Start with Hello
Linda Coles

Available in print and e-book formats

WILEY